Operative Freemasonry:

A Manual for Restoring Light and Vitality to the Fraternity

Kirk C. White

Five Gates Publishing
Bethel, Vermont
2012

First published in 2012 by
First Gates Publishing
307 Christian Hill Road
Bethel, Vermont 05032
laurelinvt@gmail.com

Printed in the United States of America

About the Author

Kirk White is a Past Master of White River Lodge #90, Past High Priest of Whitney Chapter #5 Royal Arch Masons; current Thrice Illustrious Master of Barre Council #22 Royal and Select Masters; and Senior Warden of St. Aldemar Commandery #10 Knights Templar. He is also a 32nd degree in Scottish Rite, a member of the S.R.I.C.F., and past Puissant Sovereign of St. Helena #3 Red Cross of Constantine.

At the state level, he is Past Most Excellent Grand High Priest of the Grand Chapter of Royal Arch Masons of Vermont and is serving as Illustrious Grand Lecturer for the Grand Council of Royal and Select Masters of Vermont.

He earned a Bachelor of Arts degree in the double majors of Psychology and Religion from the University of Vermont in 1984 and a Master of Arts degree in Counseling in 1996. He also did 2 years of post-graduate study in transpersonal psychology specializing in psychosynthesis, initiatic techniques, and the psychology of personal transformation and consciousness change.

He resides in Bethel, Vermont.

Sub umbra alarum tuarum YHVH.

Dedicated to all seekers of the Light, more especially to those who are also my Masonic brethren.

Contents

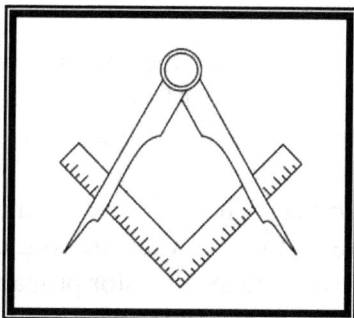

Introduction

To me, Freemasonry is one form of dedication to God and service to humanity.
- Rev. Norman V. Peale

As every new Mason learns in the second degree, there are two types of Masonry: operative and speculative. Operative masonry is the craft, knowledge and skill of building physical structures. Operative masons are those people who make practical use of their skill and knowledge of working in stone and brick. Speculative masonry – Freemasonry – is a metaphysical and spiritual system wherein the principles of geometry and the tools and practices of operative masonry are used as symbols to convey ethical and spiritual lessons so that each Mason may "by reverent and obedient conformity to the plan of the Grand Architect of the Universe, seek to attain in our lives the strength of wisdom and the beauty of virtue."

In its earliest days, joining Freemasonry was an important step for a man. Membership was hard to gain and once

1

attained, was expected to become the cornerstone around which each man built his life. A Mason's social, business and often even family contacts were strongly tied into their membership in the fraternity. Your father, uncles, brothers and cousins were members. The civic and business leaders of your community were members. Many of your customers would be members. Even the local pastor probably belonged. As a community of fraternal brothers, each member actively sought to improve the welfare of their brothers by patronizing each other's businesses, working together on community improvement projects and charities, and generally encouraging one another to live up to the tenets (brotherly love towards the whole human family, relief of suffering, truth in all dealings) and virtues (temperance, fortitude, prudence, justice) of our fraternity. The goal was to create "wise and good" men who would naturally carry that out into the world at large.

Over the last several decades, Freemasonry has gradually lost most of its effectiveness in meeting those goals. As Masonic author Cliff Porter notes, "not much if anything" in the practice of modern Freemasonry seems to be "making good men better" as is often claimed. In many cases, lodges have devolved into simple social clubs that get together to read the minutes, pay the bills, tell a few jokes and get home before the game comes on television.

Writing this book, I am operating under a number of assumptions that I feel should be stated up front.

First, that Masonry has a higher purpose than as a simple social or civic organization. As A.E. Waite wrote:

But Masonry, in my own understanding, is part of a Divine Quest; it communicates knowledge of that Quest and its terms in symbolism; while those who are willing to take the symbolism into their heart - and the innermost heart - or in other words to translate it into life, may find that it becomes an open gate into a world of real knowledge, where the Divine Quest ends in Divine Attainment.

Thus, the underlying theme of this book is that Freemasonry is a spiritual association whose primary purpose is to catalyze and facilitate that Divine Quest in its members. All of its rituals and symbols were specifically chosen or designed to fulfill that purpose. Nothing in ancient Craft Masonry is random.

Second, that the primary method used by Freemasonry to accomplish its purpose is through the use of initiation rituals. They are the primary tool for catalyzing growth in the brethren and when done properly are extremely transformative. All lodge activities either anticipate, participate or perpetuate the work done in the initiations.

Third, that Freemasonry is exceptional. That is, I believe that Freemasonry is something special. It isn't the same as the Rotary, Lions or any other civic group. Nor is it equivalent to your bowling team. It is a very specific system designed to effect the moral and spiritual transformation of its members. When done consciously and properly, it should actually change the men who join. It should set them on a lifelong journey of spiritual, moral and mental growth that the average person can't get anywhere else. Being exceptional, though, should not be confused with elitist. There are Masonic organizations that advocate many of the things I will be in the coming chapters, but they also want to limit membership via financial ability. That is, they believe that only those who can commit to a certain high level of dues should be admitted. To my mind, such elitism flies in the face of the tenet of Brother Love which states in the Vermont Monitor:

> By the exercise of Brotherly Love we are taught to regard the whole human species as one family – the high, the low, the rich, the poor – who, created by the Almighty Parent, and inhabitants of the same planet, are to aid, support and protect each other. On this principle Masonry unites men of every country, sect and opinion, and conciliates true friendship among those who might otherwise have remained at a perpetual distance.

Elitism of any sort, and especially financial, serves to maintain that perpetual distance. The only bars to admission should be moral, mental, and commitment-based and not be subject to the whim of financial fortune or misfortune.

Fourth, that in order to maintain or regain its exceptionlism, Freemasonry must have expectations on its members and its institutions. I believe that if you have zero expectations of someone, then zero is what you should expect in performance. If we actually believe and accept the exceptionalism of Freemasonry as we often say we do, then we need for our members to both be exceptional people and to treat Freemasonry as special. If someone just wants to join a group of men, there are many options out there. But if they want to join Freemasonry, we are looking for more than the right gender and the lack of a criminal record. We are looking for men who actually want to engage in the hard work of growing and changing morally and spiritually. We

4

want "doers" and not just "belongers." We also need to have expectations on those who we choose to lead our fraternity to ensure that they work to continue Freemasonry's exceptionalism.

Fifth is the importance of effective communication. Communication is a critical component in meeting the potential of our fraternity. We need to effectively communicate our exceptionalism to the world so that we can attract those kinds of "good men" that will be devoted and engaged brothers. We also need to effectively communicate our expectations to prospective members so that they know in advance what they are getting into, and once in the fraternity, what we expect of them at each state of their development. We cannot blame a brother for failure if we never told him what we wanted.

Last but in no way the least, education is the critical component to the success of the fraternity. If, as stated in the degree work, our true goal is moral and mental growth, then continued Masonic education is mandatory. To get someone through the degrees is not enough. To memorize long passages of ritual without truly understanding them is not enough. Every small detail of the three symbolic degrees of Freemasonry was put into the ritual for a specific reason. Each degree is filled with years of study and it is that study that solidifies the spiritual growth we seek. Without it, the rituals are hollow and ineffectual.

This book, therefore, is intended to be an introduction on how to "do" the kind of exceptional Freemasonry that many of us long for. It is an "operator's manual" for doing the actual work of Freemasonry, and hence the title: Operative Freemasonry.

Frontispiece. *Constitutions of the Antient Fraternity of Free and Accepted Masons containing their History, Charges, Regulations, &.* by James Anderson. A new edition by John Noorthouk. J. Rouza, London: 1784. [plate drawn by Giovanni Battista Cipriani and Paul Sandby and engraved by Francesco Bartolozzi and James Fittler.]
    Cf. Tours of Dr. Syntax by William Coombe.

6

Chapter 1: Light Defined

*Freemasonry is a science of symbols, in which, by
their proper study, a search is instituted for truth- that
truth consisting in the knowledge of the divine and
human nature, of God and the human soul.*
– Albert G. Mackey

There can be no doubt as to the specific goal of Freemasonry
– the reception of "Light." The Declaration of Principles in
Vermont state clearly that:

> To that end, it (Freemasonry) teaches and stands for
> the worship of God; truth and justice; fraternity and
> philanthropy; and *enlightenment* [emphasis mine] and
> orderly liberty, civil, religious and intellectual.

But there seems to be significant disagreement amongst the
brothers on what is meant by "Light" and "enlightenment."
The prevailing opinion seems to be that Freemasonic light are
the secrets, symbols and the moral, historical, and mythical

knowledge that are imparted. That by learning about the cardinal virtues, practicing the tenets of brotherly love, relief and truth, and taking to heart the lessons of the temple builder that this constitutes Freemasonic Light that will "make good men better." This seems to be somewhat borne out by the first degree lecture that speak of "That moral and intellectual light which emanates from the primal source of all things, the Grand Architect of the Universe, the Creator of the sun and all that it illuminates," but is that the sum of it? Moral and intellectual knowledge?

The second degree lecture seems to indicate more when it speaks of "The attainment of truth – moral and intellectual truth – and above all, that Divine truth, *the comprehension of which passeth human understanding* [emphasis mine], and to which… he can only approximate by the reception of an imperfect and yet glorious award, in the revelation of that 'light which none but Craftsmen ever saw." Further, in the prayer at the raising of a new Master Mason, the Chaplain invokes:

> Father of Light! In this dark and trying hour we humbly lift our hearts to Thee. Give our Brother, we pray Thee, that light which cometh from above…. Be Thou our light and our guide. May the lamp of Thy love dispel the gloom of the dark valley…. And in Thy glorious presence, amidst the *ineffable mysteries* [emphasis mine], be in union with the spirits of the departed in the perfect happiness of Heaven, for all eternity.

Clearly, Freemasonic Light is something more than simple moral and intellectual knowledge or the practice of brotherly love and charity. It is "ineffable"; indescribable with words.

It exceeds human understanding – beyond our mental and intellectual capacities - and can only be received through revelation.

For R.W. Bro. Michael W. Walker, Grand Secretary, Grand Lodge of Ireland, Freemasonic Light affects the recipient on a deep, psychological level so that each brother who receives it is transformed. He writes:

> The purpose of Freemasonry is "self-improvement" — not in the material sense, but in the intellectual, moral and philosophic sense of developing the whole persona and psyche so as, in the beautiful and emotive language of the ritual, "to fit ourselves to take our places, as living stones, in that great spiritual building, not made by hands, eternal in the Heavens.

These respected Masonic authors seem to be indicating that Freemasonic Light is more than lessons of morality and historical knowledge. It is some kind of mysterious Divine revelation that brings about a specific cognitive shift, a change in a person's mind and soul. And the mechanism for bringing about that Divine revelation and cognitive transformation is through the process of initiation.

Brother Albert Mackey writes:

> Light is an important word in the Masonic system. It conveys a far more recondite meaning than it is believed to possess by the generality of readers. It is in fact the first of all the symbols presented to the neophyte, and continues to be presented to him in various modifications throughout all his future progress in his Masonic career. It does not simply

mean, as might be supposed, truth or wisdom, but it contains within itself a far more abstruse allusion to the very essence of Speculative Masonry, and embraces within its capacious signification all the other symbols of the Order. Freemasons are emphatically called the Sons of Light, because they are, or at least are entitled to be, in possession of the true meaning of the symbol; while the profane or uninitiated who have not received this knowledge are, by a parity of expression, said to be in darkness.

Masonic writer A.E. Waite takes this further by stating that:

Masonry is a hieroglyphical abstract, or itinerary of the integration of the mind of God. Our initiations, passings, raisings, our exaltations and installations are stages of progress by which – ex hypothesi and figuratively – the mind of the recipient enters into light and is advanced therein.

Finally, Robert Fludd writes:

This first, best gift given by God to perfect the remainder of his construction, Moses called Light... This light, therefore, is a unique material that has substance, that exists unmixed, and is the purest, worthiest, and noblest of all; so great is its nobility indeed, that the more matter partakes of the nature of light, the more perfect and noble it is therefore considered to be.

Masonic Light, then, is Divine knowledge – a progressive raising up of one's own consciousness toward integration with the mind of God – that transforms the recipient on multiple levels including the intellectual, moral, philosophical and spiritual realms. This knowledge cannot be measured, but it can be recognized. And those brothers who have undergone that transformation is what creates "that sacred and inviolable bond which unifies men of the most discordant opinions into one band of brothers," known as the Mystic Tie.

However, enlightenment brings with it responsibility to all of God's creation. Walker points out that "Such an hypothetical whole, developed, complete person must, in his journey through life, and in his interaction with others, make a more extensive contribution to society in general, thus realizing and fulfilling his expressed wish on initiation, to become 'more extensively useful amongst his fellow-men.' Such are the lofty, lawful and laudable aspirations of the Order."

Or put another way in the Masonic Declaration of Principles:

> Through the improvement and strengthening of the character of the individual man, Freemasonry seeks to improve the community. Thus it impresses upon its members the principles of personal righteousness and personal responsibility, enlightens them as to those things which make for human welfare, and inspires them with the feeling of charity, or good will, toward all mankind which will move them to translate principle and conviction into action.

That is, as a man receives more Light and thus becomes "more perfect and noble," he will naturally be moved to shine that Light into the world around him and thus is the whole world transformed.

MASONIC EMBLEMS

Respectfully Dedicated by permission to the Most Worshipful Grand Master Mason of Scotland.
By His Humble Servant William Gray

Chapter 2: Secrets and Mysteries

It is for each individual Mason to discover the secrets of Masonry, by reflection upon its symbols and a wise consideration and analysis of what is said and one in he work. Masonry does not inculcate her truths; She states them, once and briefly; or hints them, perhaps, darkly; or interposes a cloud between them and eyes that would be dazzled by them. "Seek, and ye shall find," knowledge and the truth.
- Albert Pike

Before we go any further, a better understanding of secrets and mysteries will be useful. In Freemasonry, we often hear about the "secrets" of the Craft, and the hidden "mysteries." All of them seem tied up with the importance of the initiation – the making of a man a Mason – but the specifics of how or why is absent.

So let's explore these terms and how they all fit together:

A "secret" is simply any piece of information that is concealed from others. Once that information ceases to be concealed, it is no longer a secret.

A "mystery", as it was originally defined in ancient Greece and used in the Orphic and Eleusinian mystery schools, is a type of Divine revelation that can only be conveyed by experience and is incomprehensible to reason. The revelation *initiates* or begins a cognitive change in the recipient – also known as the initiate – that alters the way he or she sees and interacts with the world. It is not based on information or even feelings and therefore, it cannot be put into words. William James describes it as "ineffable." Schopenhauer further distinguishes the ineffability of the mysteries:

> We see all religions at their highest point end in mysticism and mysteries, that is to say, in darkness and veiled obscurity. These really indicate merely a blank spot for knowledge, the point where all knowledge necessarily ceases. Hence for thought this can be expressed only by negations, but for sense-perception it is indicated by symbolical signs, in temples by dim light and silence. In the widest sense, mysticism is every guidance to the immediate awareness of what is not reached by either perception or conception, or generally by any knowledge. The mystic is opposed to the philosopher by the fact that he begins from within, whereas the philosopher begins from without. The mystic starts from his inner, positive, individual experience, in which he finds himself as the eternal and only being, and so on. But nothing of this is communicable except the assertions that we have to accept on his word; consequently he is unable to convince.

Schopenhauer is describing that experience that all Masons say they are pursuing; "that Divine truth, the comprehension of which passeth all human understanding... the revelation of that 'light which none but Craftsmen ever saw.'"

The difference between secrets and mysteries, then, is that while both are concealed, secrets are pieces of information that can be told or explained. Secrets can be broken. The "secrets" of Freemasonry are all of the signs, grips, passwords, and the contents of our rituals. However, they, in themselves, do not constitute the "mystery" nor do they bring it about. The secrets of Freemasonry have long been published. If just reading or memorizing this information was sufficient to bring about initiation, then anyone who went online to read them would have seen the Light. This is clearly not the case.

Mysteries, on the other hand, cannot be verbally explained, which is why we have to rely so heavily on symbols and symbolic language. Anything that can be explained is not a mystery. Mysteries can only be experienced.

That is not to say that secrets have no real value in Masonry. On the contrary, they are fundamental to setting the stage for experiencing the mysteries. According to Masonic author Greer, secrets have a number of practical uses in modern day lodges. Dramatically, secrecy reinforces the effect of the ritual by maintaining an element of surprise. Familiarity breeds complacency. If we know what is going to happen, we can at least partially tune out. The element of the unknown holds and focuses the candidate's attention so that he is fully engaged and aware. Further, it enhances his levels of apprehension and disorientation, which, as we will see in

Chapter 6, are both critical components to a truly transformational initiation.

On a cognitive level, secrecy begins the breaking down of our limited worldviews necessary for true growth and change. As Greer points out, our conception and experience of the world is based on a consensus generated by everyone who communicates with us – our friends, family, media, marketing, and communities. This limited worldview is reinforced 24/7 and only by actively stepping away from it can we hope to ever have room to get a fresh perspective. It is for this reason that almost all world religions and spiritualities emphasize the benefits of solitude and retreat.

At the same time, secrecy focuses the mind on that which it is concealing and builds identification with it. If we are being constantly vigilant of everything we say in order to keep a secret, then we are spending a lot of time thinking about it. This allows the secret to sink deeply into our minds. And since we know that not everyone has the secret, it helps to create a group identity of those who have the secret and those who don't. "We" keep the secret from everyone else. This creates loyalty and group cohesion.

Further, Greer describes secrecy as "a method of reshaping the self, a discipline that transforms the relationship between the individual and the world of experience." As the candidate struggles to keep the secrets he has to cultivate introspection and self-knowledge while developing the focus, discipline and will to maintain his constant vigilance.

Lastly, secrecy opens up the mind of the candidate to the possibility of revelation and mystery. By acknowledging that there are secrets, the candidate is opened up to the potential of the unknown; that by knowing that there are actually hidden truths to be found, he is more likely to seek and experience them. Combined with his burgeoning introspection, he begins to develop the skills to find Divine Truth as revealed through his own direct experience. This direct experience is what reveals the Mystery and cannot be communicated by words. The mystery, Divine Truth, and the experiences that lead to them, are thus personal, individual and deeply subjective. Only by experiencing it one's self can it be gained, and the primary tool for providing that experience is by initiation. We'll be dissecting the mechanisms through which initiation does this in Chapter 6.

An initiation is by definition a ceremony whereby the candidate receives the mystery; the experience that brings about the Divine revelation that *initiates* the desired cognitive shift. If there was no change in cognition, no deepening of spiritual insight, no ineffable experience, then an initiation *ritual* may have been performed, but no initiation happened. A well-read and practiced brother who just went through the motions and recited the lines perfectly has not necessarily received the mystery. Mentally knowing the ritual word for word does not constitute knowing the mystery, nor does memorizing the words bring it about. Those who have had the cognitive change can recognize each other with or without secret passwords or signs.

The mysteries, unlike Masonic secrets, do not have to be kept concealed. If someone has not had the cognitive shift that comes from the mystical experience of initiation, they will not see or recognize the mysteries when they see them. Our lodges are full of them displayed for all to see. The arrangement of the lodge, the pillars, the mosaic tile, the trestleboards… all of them reveal the mysteries of

Freemasonry and are hidden in plain sight. Every single item in lodge, every symbol, every line of ritual or floorwork is embedded with multiple layers of spiritual meaning designed to transform the hearts and minds of the brothers, and yet so many brothers walk by them every month and never give a thought. They may know the secrets of Freemasonry, but they do not know the mysteries.

This is where secrets can become problematic. Too often brothers mistake the secrets for the mysteries and start focusing entirely on them rather than the initiatic process and experience. When this happens, we get the hollow recitation so common in many lodges today; and the candidates fail to receive the Light they were promised. For those brothers who joined specifically seeking spiritual development, they find disappointment and eventually seek the Light elsewhere. For those brothers who joined for fraternal bonding, they find a bunch of men dressing up in costumes muttering strangely phrased ritual lines but no emotional or spiritual bond – no moral or social virtues to cement them - and unless they receive it in their mentorship, they too will eventually desert the fraternity.

By relearning the methods of Operative Freemasonry, we can restore the mystery to our beloved fraternity and with it, our vitality and our good repute before the world.

Chapter 3: Prospective Freemasons

When the mind has entered a pious soul, it leads that soul to the light of knowledge; and such a soul is never weary of praising and blessing God, and doing all manner of good to all men by word and deed, in imitation of its Father.
– from Libellus X

If we accept the premise that Freemasonry's purpose is to bring good, upright men to Divine Light through initiation, transforming their minds and spirits to be aligned with Divine Will, and leading them to serve the greater good of all humankind, then every aspect of our lodge's activities should reflect and further those goals. This process will, therefore of necessity, begin with our prospective new members.

Who They are and How to Find Them

There was a point in time when one of the main reasons someone joined the fraternity was because of familial ties. Dad, granddad and great granddad were all Masons. In many of our lodges, that is still the number one reason why someone joins. However, we often notice that these men do not become regular attendees. As has been pointed out by others, there are lots of obligations on modern men competing for their time. Family ties often aren't enough.

Another traditional reason was fraternal and community bonding. It was a chance to meet and hang out with other men in the community. And while this is still an important reason some men join, again there are many alternatives many of which provide better opportunities for strictly community bonding. We often lose these guys to Rotary or other civic clubs.

Nonetheless, some of both these groups do stay and become active members. We don't want to overlook them. To encourage familial members, we can host Masonic "bring your son to Work" nights or other such events where they can meet other members and learn what the fraternity is about. To encourage those interested in fraternal or community bonding, host a Masonic horseshoe, golf or (for the younger men) volleyball tournament, a bowling league or such. Have an "I'm a Mason" week each year where every lodge member wears a t-shirt and puts a sign up in their business, does community improvements (such as spring street sweeping), and maybe hosts one of those tournaments. Show that Masons are present in your community, are good wholesome productive community members, and have loads of fun.

Other reasons why some men join are because they love ritual or are interested in studying and being part of the history of Masonry. To attract these men, an "open house" where there is a representative (but not actual) ritual with officers in full regalia and a short historical lecture might work.

However, the single most common reason why modern men seek out Freemasonry is spiritual growth. In his address to the 2010 General Grand Chapter Royal Arch Masons International, Robert G. Davis noted that "studies engaged in researching the needs of men in today's society are indicating that an organization that is centered on education, spiritual development and fraternal bonding may be the most powerfully compelling organization to join for men who fall within the 19 – 40 age range."

Today's young (and middle aged) men want more than just familial or civic bonding. Because of the intellectual and spiritual void left by our media, these intellectually and spiritually curious men are desirous of deeper thought and understanding, and crave active participation in a group that will give them these things. Typically, they find us through websites, social media, and Freemasonic and esoteric blogs. They are precisely the kind of men we want because they are actively seeking "moral and intellectual Light." However, this is a double-edged sword. They are all internet sophisticated and have already done their research before they even inquire about joining Freemasonry. They know what they want, and because of their research, they are knowledgeable about the alternatives and motivated enough to leave if they don't get it. We cannot get away with the "same old" that has driven brothers out of the fraternity for decades. This is where the ideas of exceptionalism, expectations communication and education come in. As you will see, these themes are woven through each stage of the process.

Information, Application, Investigation, and Commitment

Lodge candidacy processes vary fairly widely from state to state and even lodge to lodge. Some lodges take them very seriously and in others they are almost a formality to get through as quickly as possible. This latter approach often goes like this:

Old George, a long-time member and past master, wants his grandson Jimmy to join. Jimmy's father, Bill, and uncle Ted are also long-time brothers. George, Bill and Ted tell Jimmy that he ought to join this wonderful fraternity but not much else. They give him a petition, sign it as recommenders and present it to lodge. An investigating committee of people who know Jimmy is dispatched to meet with him. Because they already know him and his family, they only ask the most essential questions about faith and interest. The investigating committee reports positively, the lodge ballots in the affirmative and Jimmy is made a Mason. After four or five meetings, Jimmy is never seen in lodge again.

The problem was that Jimmy wasn't really committed to the goals of the fraternity. How could he be? He was never fully informed about what he was getting into – the fraternity's goals, methods and activities – nor what was fully expected of him. He was never really educated or challenged because the assumption was that his family would have done those things. Or out of respect for the family's service. Who wants

22

to be the one to tell Old George, Bill and Ted that Jimmy isn't right enough for the fraternity and reject his application? But family members are seldom impartial.

If we are to take our fraternity's value seriously, then we do ourselves and the candidate a huge disservice if we do not thoroughly inform the candidate of everything that he can expect from us and that we will expect of him and his family. In order to do that, three distinct phases need to be employed: Information, Application and Investigation.

Information Phase

This is the phase that is most often skimmed over, and yet it is probably the most critical. When a brother gives someone an application, there should also be a cover letter asking the potential applicant to contact the Worshipful Master to schedule a *required* informational meeting. (See example in appendices). For larger, more active lodges, these might be group meetings held every three months. Smaller lodges may hold them individually for each candidate.

At this meeting, the candidate should be given the following information:

- Clear explanation of the goals of the fraternity (moral and mental education, spiritual growth, and fraternal bonding)
- Brief history of the fraternity
- In general, what Masonic activities take place in and outside of lodge
- Expectations of the lodge
- Attendance and Time Commitment involved

- Financial costs
- Involvement in lodge functions
- Educational progress
- Attire and deportment in lodge
- What process to expect if he decides to apply
- Affirmation that to join is a serious commitment with real expectations but that to those who fulfill them, the rewards are commensurately great.
- Answers to any other questions

A full example of the above is given in the appendices. A copy should be given to the potential applicant. At the end of the informational session, the candidate should be encouraged to spend a few days reviewing the information sheet, discussing it with his wife and family, and contemplating whether or not Freemasonry is a good match for him at this time. Along with the information sheet should be an application, a petitioner questionnaire, and instructions on where and how to submit them.

The informational session serves the process of getting the "informed consent" of the candidate. Some men will decide it is too much and won't apply. That is good. We are not setting them or ourselves up for failure. On the other hand, by not sugar coating the requirements of the fraternity – in fact, by the very process of making it seem truly challenging – any man who does actually submit an application has already committed himself to the process. He has already bought in and his mental preparation for initiation is well begun.

Application Phase

This process should be fairly straightforward if the applicant has attended the required informational meeting. If he hasn't attended one yet, he should be required to before his application is acted upon. Once the informational meeting has been attended and the application and petitioner questionnaire submitted, an investigation committee should be formed who will contact the application within one week of their formation to have a meeting.

Investigation Phase

The informational meeting is for the potential applicant to learn about Freemasonry and the lodge. The investigation is for the lodge to learn about the applicant. This phase should have two components – a questionnaire and a personal interview. The petitioner questionnaire should have been given to the applicant at the informational meeting along with the petition. An example of this form is provided in the appendices. It is designed to look for objective data that may impact the lodge's decision. Such things include basic personal information (address, contact information, work place, family size), required Masonic minimums (age, faith in a Supreme Being), as well as verifiable character details such as the presence of a criminal record, history of drug or alcohol addiction, residential transience or stability, and personal references. The investigation committee should review this document prior to the interview. If any red flags are risen from it, these can be followed up at the interview or independently.

The interview is designed to examine the more subjective qualities of the applicant, his family and his home life. The interview should be done in the applicant's home with his wife or significant other present. She was not present at the informational meeting so she may have questions for you as well.

In the appendices there is a full list of potential questions to ask. These are general questions designed to explore his interest in Freemasonry and specific ones intended to turn up any red flags. Examples of general questions are:

> What have you read or heard about Freemasonry?

> There are several reasons why men join us – desire for spiritual or esoteric knowledge, interest in history, enjoyment of ritual and drama, fraternal camaraderie – what is it you hope to get out of Freemasonry?

> What is it you think you would bring to Freemasonry?

If for some reason he doesn't seem to have a good grasp on what Freemasonry is or a sincere drive to be a member, he should not be recommended.

Examples of specific questions are:

> What does your wife think about Freemasonry? Would she be okay with you being out once a week for lodge activities?

> What other clubs or organizations do you belong to? How active are you in them? If not, why not? How would Freemasonry be different?

Again, if you get a sense that his partner might not be okay with the required commitment of time, money and energy, or if he seems to be a "joiner" who then drops out a few months later, then he should not be recommended.

Once the interview is completed, the investigation committee should have a very detailed and reasonable understanding of who the applicant is and what he is seeking. It is very important that this step is not skipped or done pro forma. By following this entire lengthy process, several things are accomplished.

- full information is exchanged
- expectations are made explicit and thus, accountability can be held
- the candidate's family are also committed and involved
- the candidate and family get the sense that this is something serious and that the lodge is engaged and caring
- the lodge, having invested so much time and energy, are invested in making sure the candidate succeeds
- the candidate, having agreed to something that has been identified as "work," is invested in being active and engaged

Assuming that the candidate is found worthy, they are already well on their way towards becoming united with our unique fraternity.

Freemason's Hall, London

Illustration reproduced from *History of the Ancient and Honorable Fraternity of Free and Accepted Masons*, edited by Henry Leonard Stillson. The Fraternity Publishing Company, Boston: 1904. [page 456.]

Chapter 4: Framing the Sacred: Preparation for Lodge

To assist in the ceremonial duties of the Lodge without seeking to unfold the symbolism, is to remain satisfied with the externals only, those husks which envelope and protect the grain. Our quest is to ascertain the internal truths of which symbolism is but the index. For instance, to what extent are the fraternal relations between my fellow Freemasons and myself different to those which I hold with my neighbours and friends?
- J. E. Thomas

One could easily argue that ritual is the primary activity of Freemasonry. We open our meetings with ritual. We have rituals for funerals, dedicating new lodges, and installing our officers. And of course, our main ritual activity is the initiation of brothers to the various degrees of Freemasonry. If we aren't actively engaged in ritual, we are preparing to do so. So let's look at what ritual really is and how it works.

According to professor of religion, William Paden,

> Ritual is the deliberate structuring of action and time
> to give focus, expression, and sacredness to what
> would otherwise be diffuse, unexpressed, or profane.
> Ritual is sacred action and time deliberately created.
> Like any behavior, ritual can degenerate into a
> mechanical act. But in its essential nature it is an act
> of concentrated display with regard to some particular
> purpose. Ritual time is the specialized instance taken
> for granted but operative in all experience – namely,
> the difference between concentrative and
> nonconcentrative time. Ritual builds its realms on the
> force of this distinction. The mind can be inattentive,
> diluted, spread out; but it can also attach itself to
> special projects with unalloyed attention and
> acuteness of focus. What is implicit is made explicit.
> All ritual behavior gains its basic effectiveness by
> virtue of such undivided, intensified concentration and
> by bracketing off distraction and interference.

What Paden is saying is that part of what makes an action a
ritual as opposed to any other thing you do is the deliberate
setting apart of that time and action – making it special.
Conversely, doing something special builds attention and
focus, the building blocks of ritual.

Simply put, a ritual is an established or prescribed set of
behaviors. Most often we think of them for religious
purposes but people use rituals every day in ordinary ways.
Many people have a morning and a bedtime ritual. The
morning ritual – get up, go the bathroom, let the dog out, start
the coffee, take a shower, get dressed, have breakfast or
whatever your ritual is – is what we use to organize our

thoughts and get mentally focused for the day ahead. It might differ depending on whether it is a workday or not, but many people find that if their morning ritual is disrupted then their whole day is thrown off. At bedtime, the ritual helps to unwind and quiet the mind for sleep. In all of those cases, the purpose of ritual is to alter the mental state of the ritualist so that some kind of transition can happen.

In religious ceremonies, the same process applies. The established ritual is designed to focus the minds of the participants on God, create an altered state, and open the possibility of spiritual growth. Ritual causes mental change and that is its purpose.

How ritual accomplishes that change is by bracketing the time spent as "special" and unlike our ordinary, mundane lives. By doing a special set of behaviors unlike those in the rest of your day or life, we mark that time as unique. Weddings and holidays are "special" because they involve special established behaviors - we wear special clothes, have special ceremonies, eat special food, sing special songs, do special dances, and so forth.

Masonic ritual is not an exception. Our opening and closing rituals mark the time in lodge as different from our daily lives. Just being in a special time and place begins to alter the way our minds work. Then because the purpose of the fraternity is to ultimately make its votaries wiser and more spiritually developed – "enlightened" – our members are exposed through lectures and initiations to special symbols and concepts to allow for a connection to the Divine – the Great Architect of the Universe. The opening ritual is critical. It makes the actual transmission and integration of the lessons of Masonry possible. Otherwise Masonry would be no different than a philosophical book club. Let us look at other ways in which lodges can and do affect the mental state necessary for ritual.

Due Signs and Summons

The first step bracketing out lodge time as special, and thus beginning the process of mental preparation necessary to have actual ritual, is in the invitation. In our daily lives, we do not receive formal invitations very often. Typically, they are sent for big events – weddings, christenings, big anniversaries, special parties. Therefore, to receive an invitation or "summons" to attend lodge marks it as unique.

Additionally, each Mason has taken a solemn oath to answer "all due signs and summons." As stated before, we need to start having expectations for members. As per their oaths, they should be required to attend all meetings unless they have good reason not to. If they cannot, they should be expected to call the secretary and explain why not. They made a commitment, why do we not make them stick to it? Our new members see that meeting attendance isn't valued by the rest of the lodge or chapter, so why should they value it?

Lastly, by actually receiving a summons, each brother is reminded on a monthly basis of the oath and obligations he has taken. On a mental level, he is already beginning to reconnect with the fraternity. On a more practical note, how can we hold and enforce our expectation that members keep their oath by attending lodge meetings if we never actual summon them? Therefore, the monthly sending of summons to all lodge members, by mail or by email, is very important.

Changing Your Clothes Can Change Your Mind

As with all other special events in our lives, an important part of the ritual is the preparation that takes place before a brother even leaves for lodge. Before a wedding, a funeral, church or even going out for a party on New Year's Eve, the participants usually put on special clothes. Before going to work, many folks put on their "work clothes" – some kind of specialized uniform for their task ahead. Putting on the special clothes puts you into a different frame of mind. It changes your consciousness. It delineates the special from the ordinary; the sacred from the profane.

When a martial artist puts on his white gi, a basketball player puts on his uniform and laces his shoes, or a boxer wraps his hands, he is changing his mental state. He begins to gear up for the match ahead. His mind focuses, his concentration intensifies, and he becomes more serious about the work ahead. The process of preparing for the ritual *is* a ritual in itself.

Preparing for lodge is no different. We are preparing for spiritual work. It is a special activity; a sacred activity. We open in the name of God and seek his blessings and guidance in all of our undertakings. It is serious work. It doesn't have to *always* be solemn, but it should always be serious.

Thus, our preparations for lodge should be serious. If we wear to lodge what we would wear around the house, we fail in our preparations. We are not taking it seriously. We are not making it special. We are not preparing our minds for further Light and thus, we shouldn't be surprised that so many of our brethren never actually get any. They get fellowship and a good time, but not so much of the spiritual growth and maturity. Special dress is a way of actually doing the work of Masonry, of smoothing our own rough ashlars.

Further, special dress for lodge is an act of respect – to our God, our brothers, and to ourselves. To our God in that we usually wear special clothes for other times when we invoke Him, in churches and other religious ceremonies such as weddings and funerals. Why do we not do so at lodge? To our brothers in showing them that our brotherly love and friendship is real and it is special. We would wear a suit out of respect to a brother's funeral, yet we can't wear one while he's alive? Or more importantly, when we raise him to brotherhood? And to ourselves, in respecting ourselves to be duly and truly prepared - physically and mentally - to actually engage in the lodge ritual work in the way in which it was intended: solemnly and sincerely. For only in such a prepared state where we have consciously "tended to every particular" can the work of the lodge actually "render all men."

Attitude is Everything

Because ritual is built by concentration, focus, and the "bracketing off of distraction and interference," our mental attitude before and during lodge plays a large part in whether or not our actions are actually ritual, and thus able to elicit the experiential impact necessary for actual initiation, or simply a "mechanical act."

Throughout the Masonic Monitor and floorwork are admonishments to the brothers to act solemnly and seriously during ritual work or even open lodge. In the Ancient Charges it is written:

> In the lodge while constituted you are not to hold private committees, or separate conversation, without leave from the Master, nor to talk of anything impertinent or unseemly, nor interrupt the Master or Wardens, or any Brother speaking to the Master; nor behave yourself ludicrously or jestingly while the Lodge is engaged in what is serious and solemn.

Idle chatter on the sidelines during ritual, joking around during the ritual – and especially during initiations – serve to diffuse the concentration and focus necessary to have effective ritual. Brothers who engage in these activities are preventing the candidate from have actual initiatic experiences and the concurrent cognitive changes necessary to actually become aware of the hidden mysteries of Freemasonry. Sadly, this behavior frequently arises because those very brothers did not themselves have an actual initiation because their initiators likewise lacked the necessary focus. And thus through a succession of ages, rather than passing on the mysteries of Masonry, these lodges have perpetuated the hollow shell of mechanical ritual that so often is not enough to keep brothers engaged and coming to lodge.

That is not to say that going to lodge shouldn't be fun. The Ancient Landmarks are again clear: "Behavior after the Lodge is Over and the Brethren not Gone: You may enjoy yourselves with innocent mirth, treating one another according to ability, but avoiding all excess, or forcing any Brother to eat or drink beyond his inclination…" The jokes and fun are supposed to happen after lodge, not during. Prior to lodge, the brethren should be mentally preparing themselves.

Lodge Greeting

If one of the things that new brothers are seeking is fraternal bonding, then when people are arriving at lodge, it is very important that each and every brother be properly greeted. This is even more critical of visiting brothers. It is not uncommon for a visiting brother to not feel like a brother, but rather, like he is at someone else's family reunion. The officers are busy getting things ready and the members are catching up with one another. All the while, the visiting brother stands off to the side by himself waiting for the opening. He can stand there a whole half hour and not have someone talk to him and if they do, it is only to say "hello," shake his hand and move on. For extroverts, this isn't a problem. They approach others and leap into a conversation. But for introverts, it can feel very isolating and unfriendly. And let's be aware that a certain percentage of men who join Masonry, especially the kinds of brothers who join looking for education and deep spiritual development more than fraternal bonding, are often introverts.

If any brother, visiting, newly initiated, or regular attendee feels ungreeted and left out – that is, he doesn't feel brotherly love – then this is a barrier to his being able to feel the comfort necessary to be fully present and focused during lodge. His experience of lodge will suffer and overtime, his discomfort may lead him to stop coming.

The solution is for each lodge to have at least one person designated as their greeter. Traditionally this job fell to the Senior Warden as he vetted members but it doesn't have to be him. But *someone* should meet every new member or visitor, introduce them around before the opening, and stay with them until they find someone to converse and hang out with. If they don't find anyone, then the greeter must be that person. The greeter should also make a point of welcoming and chatting with each and every brother who arrives. This is a great job for new brothers. Perhaps every new brother should be required to serve in this role for three to six months. Multiple greeters would be fine. This would give the new member a sense of purpose in coming, would serve to deepen their fraternal bonding and integration into the lodge, and ensure that all men present experience the brotherly love we tout so strongly in our rituals.

Preparation of Candidates

The information, application, and investigation are all important parts of the preparation of candidates. As mentioned earlier, it conveys to the candidate the importance of the undertaking, gets his mental and emotional buy-in, and builds excitement. All of these things combine to begin to alter his consciousness even before the day of the initiation. Every experience he has with the lodge leading up to the actual ritual should reinforce that state. As a candidate, there are really only four situations in which this reinforcement can be done:
- invitation/ summons
- transportation
- greeting
- changing and waiting

We've already discussed the importance of a summons and proper greeting for brothers. For all of those same reasons, each of these is even more important for the new candidate. On a psychospiritual level, a summons brackets the event out as something special and it builds anticipation. Each of these contributes to ensuring that the initiation ritual has sufficient impact to be truly transformative. On a practical level, a summons makes sure that he remembers the time and date, and is introduced at the onset of his membership to the notion that he will be regularly summoned and is expected to attend. The first greeting that the candidate receives should similarly model how the lodge greets all of its brothers and guests. This is especially true if the lodge requires its new brothers to serve as greeters for a time.

Transportation to the lodge is another area where lodge members can impact the candidate's experience prior to initiation. In many lodges it is customary for the candidate's sponsor to pick him up and bring him to lodge on the nights of his initiations. The practical reasons for this are to make sure that he doesn't get lost, show up late or chicken out. Ritually, being transported to the lodge has a strong mental impact. It takes a certain amount of trust and faith to make oneself vulnerable in that way. By getting into the car, he is giving over his ability to leave if the ritual becomes too uncomfortable. He is at the mercy of (at least some) strangers who will be performing some unknown ritual on him. That can be scary and that is a good thing. As we will see in a later chapter, the heightened awareness that is generated by his fear, combined with this faith and courage to do it anyway, are two parts of the glue that make initiations transformative rather than simply a curiosity.

Lastly, once the candidate has been summoned, picked up, driven to lodge and properly greeted, he has to sit and wait while lodge is opened. This should be a solemn event. He should be escorted to a dimly lit anteroom by the Tyler, directed to sit in silence and await the ritual. To reemphasize, the candidate is already in a heightened state of excitement and fear. To sit in silence and wait will build his anticipation and further enhance his already altered state of consciousness. It is opening his mind so that he will be more acutely aware of the symbols, images and words that he will encounter. If instead his Tyler sits and idly chats or makes jokes with him while waiting, then the process becomes not much different than waiting in line at the Department of Motor Vehicles and the effect is diminished. Conversely, the effect is enhanced in those lodges that still use the traditional Chamber of Reflection – a candlelit room with various esoteric symbols including an hourglass, mirror, skull, and other mystic items. Mark Stavish writes:

> There, isolated from the profane world, alone with our thoughts, our conscience, and our consciousness, we can enter into a twilight land between self and Self for communication with our "Inner Master." This "Master" is nothing other than the spark of the Divine within us that thoughtfully and carefully has laid out a plan for our Return to Unity from which we came.

Stavish goes on to state that the Chamber of Reflection's "employment is very appropriate, for, as Gaedicke well observes, 'It is only in solitude that we can deeply reflect upon our present or future undertakings, and blackness, darkness, or solitariness, is ever a symbol of death. A man who has undertaken a thing after mature reflection seldom turns back.'"

Michael Maier (1568?-1622), *Atalanta fugiens, hoc est, Emblemata nova de secretis naturae chymica : accomodata partim oculis & intellectui, figuris cupro incisi, adiectisque sententiis, epigrammatis & notis, partim auribus & recreationi animi plus minus 50 fugis musicalibus trium vocum, quarum duae ad unam simplicem melodiam distichis canendis peraptam, correspondeant, non absq; singulari jucundiatate videnda, legenda, meditanda, intelligenda, dijudicanda, canenda & audienda/* authore Michaele Majero Imperiel. Consistorii Comite, Med. D. Equ. ex. &c Publisher: Oppenheimii : Ex typographia Hieronymi Galleri, sumptibus Joh. Theodori de Bry, MDCXVIII [1618] Physical desc.: 211, [5] p : ill. (metal cuts; woodcut)

Chapter 5: Openings and Closings

Knock on yourself as upon a door, and walk upon yourself as on a straight road. For if you walk on the road, it is impossible for you to go astray. And if you knock with this one (Wisdom), you knock on hidden treasures. – Sylvanus

The formal opening and closing rituals are what define "being in lodge." As each newly minted Master Mason learns, lodge is "open" only when certain objects are in their proper place on the altar. An assembly of Masons, even in the lodge room, who have not performed the necessary steps to open lodge are just brothers who happen to be in the same place. Therefore, the opening and closing rituals are critical to the functioning of the lodge. And yet, a number of lodges do the absolute minimum – if even that – to open and close their lodges. Then these same lodges wonder why lodge enthusiasm is low and attendance is dropping.

In order to fully understand the importance of these ceremonies, we need to remember two things:

1) that the ultimate purpose is to promote the growth of Light amongst the members
2) the importance of ritual bracketing on the mental state of the participants

As we have shown, each stage up to the opening of the lodge should be part of the preparatory bracketing of each brother. From receiving his summons, to dressing for lodge, to being greeted upon arrival and the general tenor of the group, each step should be focused on the importance of the event he is about the participate in; no less than the advancement of his connection with the Grand Architect of the Universe and his own spiritual development. That development taking the form of growth of his own moral, mental, philosophical and spiritual Light followed by the lodge's work to bring that Light to the world at large in the form of living its tenets and principles.

Therefore, the opening ritual work marks the culmination of the preparation and bracketing process. When we open the lodge, we are consciously separating ourselves from the outside, everyday world. We have passwords and signs to keep non-members out. We seal and guard the door. We wear special dress, use specialized phrases, and interact in a stylized manner. We emphasize that, unlike outside those doors, inside lodge we are all brothers and equals in a "sacred retreat of friendship and virtue."

It is the opening of the lodge ritual that unites us into "one sacred band or society of friends and Brothers." It is this ceremony that is intended to harmonize our minds and spirits. It does this through three ways:

1) emphasizing exclusivity
2) reinforcing or reawakening common language and symbols
3) entrainment

Exclusivity

As we will see in the chapter on initiation, an important component of group cohesion is a sense of the group as distinct from all other groups. It is hard to have a strong emotional connection to a group if everyone is a member. It is the sense of being "special" that both makes people want to be members and then keeps them as proud, active members. The very exclusivity expressed in the opening ritual's barring of cowans, combined with the specialized words and phrases used (e.g. cowan) grant a feeling of belonging to a special, exclusive group which reinforces cohesion.

Common Language and Symbols

Language and symbols are what structure our thoughts. According to the Sapir-Whor hypothesis, people experience the world based on the grammatical structures of their language. The example commonly given is that the speakers of different languages may see different numbers of colored bands in a rainbow. A rainbow is actually a continuum of color without definite empirical bands so the bands of colors you see are only those colors that your language has names for. And not all languages and cultures see all the same colors. Thus, the structure of the language controls how empirical data is organized and thereby the concepts we are capable of grasping or creating.

As we will see in the chapter on initiation, part of the process of cognitive change involves retraining our language and symbols. During the opening ritual, the major symbolic themes are reiterated, specialized words and unique grammatical phrasings are used, and ritualized movements are employed. Each of these serves to help switch the brothers' mental states from their day-to-day lives to their Masonic personae.

Entrainment

Entrainment is when the brainwave frequencies of two or more brains synchronize. Our brains and bodies synchronize with others all the time. A couple on a first date will synchronize brainwaves, breathing, and heart rates if they are attracted to each other. We synchronize with our friends and coworkers. It happens daily naturally and is part of what allows us to feel comfortable and work harmoniously "in sync" with one another. Entrainment can also be induced. The most common ways are through synchronized movements, rhythms or breathing. It can also be accomplished through having people watching movement together. General examples include group tai chi or yoga, dancing, shamanic drumming, team sport warm-up drills, group recitation of prayer, and singing or chanting together. In the Masonic opening ritual we see it in the synchronized movements of standing and sitting, group recitation of prayer and pledge of allegiance, and group watching of the circumambulations and floorwork.

Hopefully it is clear that none of these techniques – exclusivity, language, entrainment – are uncommon or nefarious in any way. They are the exact methods that we use unconsciously when we join any distinct group, from being a fan of a sports team, a member of a church group, or even a family through marriage. We feel special for being a part of the group often wearing special identifying clothes like team jerseys, choir robes, or religious jewelry. We start to learn the specialized language – for example "touch down" – and the inside jokes. And we entrain as we work, cheer, sing or do any other activity together. It is a large part of how humans create group cohesion. The difference is that the more consciously we use these natural techniques, the better we as Freemasons can be at getting the maximal level of unity and harmony and ultimately, of helping each other in our quest for Divine attainment.

Therefore, if all the preparatory work has been done by each brother beforehand, the opening ritual is designed to take their individual states of focus and unite them into one harmonized group focused on the attainment of Light through the symbols and concepts invoked during the opening. This then sets the stage for the ritual or educational work to be done that evening. At the end, the closing ritual serves as reminder to then take the Light out into their daily lives. As it says in the closing prayer in the Vermont Monitor:

> Forget not the duties to which you have heard so
> frequently inculcated and forcibly recommended in
> the Lodge.... Finally, Brethren, be ye all of one mind;
> live in peace; and may the God of love and peace
> delight to dwell with and bless you.

VIDE, AUDE, TACE.

5776.

Published according to Act of Parliament Aug.t 30. 1776 by G. Nicoll.

46

Chapter 6: Initiation

*The practice of the Hermetic/Kabbalistic Tradition of
the Renaissance was an interior ascent, and when one
"turns inside," one finds himself in the domain that
we call the psyche. This was as true for the
philosopher of the Renaissance as it is for us today.
As Carl Jung demonstrated in his work, Psychology
and Alchemy, the intellectual community of the
Renaissance studied the psyche; they simply had a
very different purpose than that of our contemporary
psychologists who seek to help people adapt to life in
the physical world.*
- W. Kirk MacNulty

As Freemasons, we perform and receive initiations all the
time. As I have argued earlier, stimulation of Light in the
minds and psyches of its members is the primary purpose of
our fraternity. I have also asserted that initiations are the
primary method through which Masonry brings its brothers to
Light. So let's explore what initiations are, where our form

of initiation originated, and how they bring about the desired effect.

Definitions

The word "initiation" comes from the Latin initi(um) which literally means "beginning." Therefore, at its most basic meaning, "initiation" simply refers to commencing a new endeavor. More specifically, however, the dictionary defines "initiation" as the introduction into the secret knowledge of some art or subject or formal admission into a society, club, or group that keeps such knowledge. One could certainly argue that a Freemasonic initiation does in fact mark formal admission into the fraternity; that the new Mason does indeed commence on a new endeavor and that endeavor includes secret knowledge. So on the most perfunctory level, initiation is simply joining the fraternity and, unfortunately, a significant number of brothers just leave it at that.

However, as William Preston noted in a speech on May 21, 1772: "Many have been deluded by the vague supposition that the mysteries of masonry were merely nominal, that the practices established among us were slight and superficial, and that our ceremonies were of such trifling import, as to be adopted or waved at pleasure." There is more to Freemasonic initiation than just a formal entry ritual.

Noted professor of religion, Mircea Eliade wrote:

> The term initiation in the most general sense denotes a body of rites and oral teachings whose purpose is to produce a decisive alteration in the religious and

48

social status of the person to be initiated. In philosophical terms, initiation is equivalent to a basic change in existential condition: the novice emerges from the ordeal endowed with a totally different being from that which he possessed before his initiation; he has become another.

Therefore, underneath the "nominal" effects of simple admission to the fraternity, initiation is intended to actually change the candidate; a rebirth with a new cognitive frame that allows him to see that he could not before – to behold the "mysteries" of Freemasonry and not just the secrets. Brother W.L. Wilmhurst confirms this as the purpose of Freemasonic initiation when he writes:

> The purpose of Initiation may be defined as follows: - it is to stimulate and awaken the Candidate to direct cognition and irrefutable demonstration of facts and truths of his own being about which previously he has been either wholly ignorant or only notionally informed; it is to bring him into direct conscious contact with the Realities underlying the surface-images of things, so that, instead of holding merely beliefs or opinions about himself, the Universe and God, he is directly and convincingly confronted with Truth itself; and finally it is to move him to become the Good and the Truth revealed to him by identifying himself with it.

Freemasonry speaks of "making good men better" and of "rending all men who conform to its precepts." How this is done is not simply through learning some old rituals, hanging out with brothers, and giving lip service to our tenets, principles and ethics. It can only really happen when we fundamentally change the way our brothers see, think, and act in the world. Initiation – when done properly - is the process through which this is accomplished.

Antecedents

> From this school we derive… the system of symbolism and allegory which lay at the foundation of the Masonic philosophy. To no ancient sect, indeed, except perhaps to the Pythagoreans, have the Masonic teachers been so much indebted for the substance of their doctrines, as well as the esoteric method of communicating them, as that of the School of Alexandria.

From Brother Mackey's statement above, there is little doubt that the symbols and ritual forms used by our fraternity are strongly influenced by the Greek Mystery schools. Despite his assertion, they are not direct descendents from these schools - that is, we are not part of some unbroken lineage from these schools to the present - but the Greek Mystery schools were influential on our symbols and rituals nonetheless. C. Bruce Hunter points out that:

> During the early years of the Grand Lodge period it was widely believed that the fraternity had at least some historic connections with the mystery religions (sometimes called "mysteries" for short). Today almost everyone agrees that such a connection never existed. In other words, the modern fraternity did not descend from the mysteries. But this doesn't mean there wasn't any connection. The very name "mystery religion" demands a closer look, because in religious

circles the word "mystery" is defined as "a hidden reality or secret." This is precisely what the masonic lodge offers its members, which in itself suggests something worth investigating. Moreover, the mere fact that early masonic historians were convinced of a connection suggests that something was afoot.

In a 1996 article, W. Kirk MacNulty notes that "Speculative Masonry, in the sense that we understand the term today, seems to appear first in the early-to-mid-seventeenth century. This is the period that marks the end of the Renaissance in England and Northern Europe." MacNulty goes on to suggest that our modern ritual is essentially a distillation of Renaissance thought culminating in the finishing details of Calcutt, Hutchinson and Preston in 1772. For as Hunter asserts: "While there is no reason to believe the lodge actually descended from the mystery religions, the men who created Freemasonry were certainly aware of the mysteries."

So what are these "mysteries"? The Greek Mysteries were religious groups that held dramatic rituals that were reserved to initiates. The most popular and famous of these groups were the Eleusinian Mysteries which began prior to the Greek Dark Ages (c. 1500 BC) and reached its peak of popularity in the Late Antiquity of the fourth century AD. According to Plato, "the ultimate design of the Mysteries… was to lead us back to the principles from which we descended… a perfect enjoyment of intellectual (spiritual) good." According to Taylor:

> The dramatic shows of the Lesser Mysteries occultly signified the miseries of the soul while in subjection to the body, so those of the Greater obscurely intimated, by mystic and splendid visions, the felicity

of the soul both here and hereafter, when purified from the defilements of a material nature and constantly elevated to the realities of intellectual [spiritual] vision.

These descriptions show the strong influence of Platonic and Neoplatonic thought that eventually became major themes in the Mysteries. As we will see, Neoplatonic thought would reassert its influence on our Renaissance brethren who contributed to the formation of our rites.

At the time of the evolution of Freemasonry, the Renaissance was in full swing. According to MacNulty,

> The Renaissance is usually thought of as an explosion of art. It was certainly that; but it was very much more. Its philosophy was based on Judeo-Christian monotheism; but it was also characterized by a revival of interest in the Classical world and its thought (in particular Greek and Roman civilizations) and by a strong neo-Platonic influence. Medieval scholars had been interested in classical philosophy from the point of view of reconciling it to Christian doctrine. Renaissance scholars were interested in classical philosophy for what it said about man, himself. These Renaissance philosophers incorporated a good many Greek (particularly neo-Platonic) and Jewish mystical ideas into their orthodox thought.

Renaissance philosophy was strongly influenced by two primary sources: the Hermetica and the Kabbalah. The Hermetica were a number of Greek wisdom texts written around Alexandria in the second and third centuries CE. A combination of early Christian, Egyptian and Hellenized

Judaic thought, these texts were lost to Western culture during the Middle Ages. With Europe's increased exposure to the libraries of the Byzantine Empire, they were rediscovered in 1460, translated into Latin by Marsilio Ficino in 1471 and later into English in 1650. Many of the most influential philosophers of the age, including Giordano Bruno and Ficino's student, Pico della Mirandola were strongly influenced by the Hermetica.

The Kabbalah is a mystical tradition of esoteric Rabbinic Judaism. Although its origins are lost in antiquity and are generally considered to be a confluence of developments over millennia, Kabbalistic thought was generally unified sometime around the twelfth century. In 1492 with the expulsion of all Jews from Spain, Kabbalistic teachings were spread throughout the Mediterranean where they too were picked up by philosophers of the time and fused with Hermetic thought.

MacNulty goes on to posit that:

> After these two influences had been interpreted in the context of orthodox Christian doctrine, the Hermetic/ Kabbalistic Tradition was fundamental to the philosophy of the early Renaissance. While it was subsequently repudiated by Counter-Reformation writers, it remained the essential core of Renaissance thought.... As we have said, Speculative Masonry dates from the end of the Renaissance, and it seems to me that Freemasonry is actually a codification of this thought that was at the core of the Renaissance.

He breaks down this Renaissance philosophical view into four primary concepts:

- Neoplatonism
- Correspondences/ Macrocosm vs. Microcosm
- Heavenly hierachies
- The necessity of revelation

Pertaining to Neoplatonic thought, MacNulty writes:

> The Deity was considered to be without limit. Rather
> than thinking of the Deity as creator - which must
> necessarily be separate from its creation and is, in that
> respect, limited – the neo-Platonist understand Deity
> to have projected Itself into existence as the entire
> universe. This results in a view of all existence as a
> single, tightly integrated unity centered on the Deity.
> A particularly straightforward statement of this view
> comes from the Hermetica: "...for God contains all
> things, and there is nothing that is not in God, and
> nothing which God is not. Nay, I would rather say, not
> that God contains all things, but that, to speak the full
> truth, God is all things."

MacNulty describes the concept of correspondences in terms
of the Hermetic axiom from the Emerald Table - "as above,
so below." He goes on to explain all things and events on
earth are reflections of events in the heavenly realms because,
"In a universe regarded as a single, consistent, and Divine
Entity, there must be a correspondence between that which
occurs in the higher (psychological/ spiritual) levels and that
which occurs at the lower (earthly) ones." This idea is
extended to the entire universe, called the "macrocosm," as
well as to humanity, called the "microcosm," since both are
"in the image of God."

However, these correspondences are linked in the "Great Chain of Being" that while tying all realms of the microcosm and macrocosm, also separates them into various levels of higher and lower, each reflecting the other and comprised of contrasting forces – the celestial hierarchies. These levels are the Elemental, Celestial, Super-Celestial/ Angelic and Divine realms.

Lastly, Divine knowledge or Light can only be gained through personal experience and revelation of the Divine and not through logic, information or faith alone.

These were the philosophical assumptions that were held during the earlier formulations of our institution. As Hunter points out, with the strong influence of Neoplatonic thought in these early formulations, it is no wonder that our early rituals had enough similarities to what was known of the Greek mystery traditions (religious but outside of mainstream religion, use of elaborate, highly symbolic initiatic dramas dealing with death and resurrection, solemn oaths of secrecy) that our eighteenth-century brothers believed themselves to be direct descendents of those mysteries and fashion our modern ritual accordingly. Hunter goes on to state:

> When the gentlemen Masons of the 18th century put their new ritual together, they were dealing with the same age-old questions the mystery religions had dealt with. And they chose to answer them in a similar way. Their ritual is merely a retelling of the same [theme] that lies at the heart of the mystery religions. But why such a strong affinity between the ritual and the ancient mysteries? In the final analysis, it was the unique nature of the mysteries that made them an ideal model. While the mainstream religions of the

modern world — Judaism, Islam and Christianity — rely on exegesis (i.e., explaining and interpreting the "truth"), Greek religious thought was always based on myth (i.e., dramatizing the "truth"). In other words, it used allegory to give meaning to elusive truths that cannot be fully explained in more straightforward ways. And one peculiar outgrowth of Greek religious thought, the mysteries, treated the most central and universal truths in a way that was tailor made for the kind of ritual the gentlemen Masons were creating at the dawn of the 18th century.

As we stated earlier, a "mystery" is a type of Divine revelation that can only be conveyed by experience and is incomprehensible to reason. The revelation *initiates* or begins a cognitive change in the recipient – also known as the initiate – that alters the way he or she sees and interacts with the world. It is not based on information or even feelings and, therefore, it cannot be put into words. This is what our rituals and symbols were designed to elicit. It is the purpose of our initiation rituals.

How Initiations Work

Developmental Stages

In order for us to understand how a person is "reborn," it is necessary that we understand the basics of human psychosocial development. A number of authors and psychological theorists have proposed models for human development. The following is based on theorist Ken Wilber's Integral Psychology, which synthesizes the works of his predecessors including Freud, Maslow, Piaget, Loevinger,

Erikson, Kohlberg, Fromm, Gilligan and Maslow. Some of these models break human development into dozens of stages and sub-stages. For simplicity's sake, we will focus on Maslow's six stages with elaboration from Wilber's system when useful.

Human consciousness development is initially a process of expansion and increased differentiation. This process is a continuum, growing a little each day. And each person grows at his own rate. So while we will be talking about distinct stages, please remember that there is no radical shift from one stage to the other – turning one off and one on. Instead, these will flow into one another over time. Nonetheless, there are major features of each stage that can be useful for our discussions.

The first stage is called the Survival stage. When an infant is newly born, it has very little awareness outside of its need to eat, breathe and excrete waste. Its primary focus is on its physiological survival. It's sphere of awareness to its own bodily comfort or discomfort, and just a few feet around it to determine if food is nearby. It does not have a sense of itself as an individual, social conventions, language or conceptual thinking. It is completely vulnerable and physical survival is its sole motivation.

The second stage is called the Safety stage. As the child grows, its ability to perceive and interact with the world increases. It begins to discover its own body and to differentiate between itself and "other." Around the age of two, this is exhibited with their realization that as an individual they are separate from their parents and can have an independent opinion by saying "no." They are just beginning to develop words but haven't really developed language yet. This is when young children begin to explore their worlds, pushing past the previous boundaries (e.g. their playpen) and then rushing back to momma for reassurance. This is also when they begin to be afraid of strangers. As the child begins to recognize that he exists as a distinct entity and that other entities exist that can cause him pain, safety becomes the primary issue for the child.

The third stage is called the Belonging or Membership stage. Eventually, the child begins to develop a sense of belonging to ever expanding groups. Starting at home but really taking off once in school, this is where they learn the specialized language and cultural expectations of their group or community. They learn the proper ways to dress, gender roles, acceptable and unacceptable social behavior, basic concepts and symbols. As they get older, they may join subgroups within their culture and community, each with its own more specialized language and behaviors. For example, as a Northeastern U.S. student, a child would learn English, the American flag and basic myths and stories about our country (e.g. Washington's cherry tree). They might also learn stories and behaviors about their state and town. For example, a Vermont child's learned ideas on gay marriage might be different than a South Carolina child's. Within the community, there would be different religious denominations each with their own symbol systems, specialized language (e.g. eucharist or satsang) and behaviors. Further, that child might belong to a sports team which would also have its own team colors, mascot, specialized language (e.g. "home run"), and rules. Each of these things help to have membership in and a feeling of belonging to a unique group separate from all other groups. This is a tribal mentality ("my group, right or wrong!") that helps the child develop a sense of self in context. That is, they now define themselves by their groups:

"I'm a Methodist. I live in Plaintown, Vermont where I play baseball for the Blue Star little league team. My dad is a car mechanic and I want to be one too someday so that I can change brake pads." Locales, religion, family, teams, hobbies… each helps define your membership self.

The fourth stage is called the Self-Esteem or Egoic stage. Once a child develops a sense of identity based on his or her membership, then the battle for pecking order begins. It starts early in elementary school, really starts to kick in by middle school, and lasts for the rest of most people's adult lives. This is the stage where individuals know what group they belong to, and now want to get ahead in that group and earn the respect of their peers. It is not enough to just belong; now they want to succeed.

The fifth stage is called the Existential or Self-Actualization stage. Not everyone reaches this stage and most do not until they are in late adulthood or retirement. This typically is attained when someone has succeeded to such a degree that they no longer need to strive and struggle to establish their place in the world. They have reached a place where they can break away from the rules set by others and can begin to live and act more authentically, writing their own rules for behavior and belief. Often this leads to an expanded awareness how limiting our original thinking was and a search for deeper, wider truths.

The sixth stage is called the Transpersonal stage. This person has developed a deep awareness and experience of the Divine. Because this revelation is outside of the concepts, symbols and even language of the groups that defined their thoughts and ideas, these insights are ineffable or post-verbal. They cannot be described or taught through language. That is why the mystery schools and Freemasonry just call it "the Light" and why they cannot be attained through organized religion. It is entirely experiential and revelatory. This awareness then motivates the recipient to continue seeking for more Light and to reorganize his world to support the Divine Will.

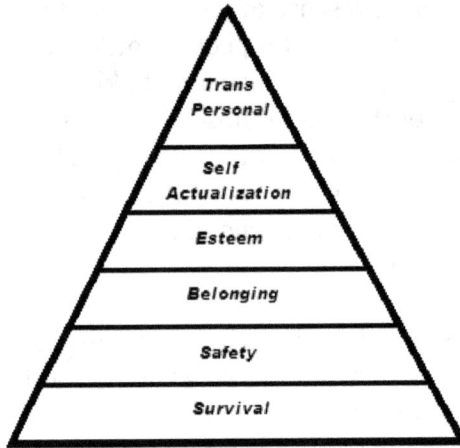

Maslow's Hierarchy of Needs

Each person who has ever lived beyond childhood has gone through this process at least to the Egoic stage. It is how we develop our worldviews, concepts, and beliefs and because we seldom interact completely outside of our culture of origin, we seldom change them. If we encounter something extremely foreign or contrary to our worldview, we often ignore it, fear it, or judge it as wrong, or occasionally we will find a way to make it fit somehow into what we already believe. For example, if I'm a strong Christian and I run into a Ganesh (Hindu elephant-headed God) worshipper I'm likely to conclude that the poor Hindu is wrong (or worse, misled by Satan), or that Ganesh is just a "myth" or story (compared to my own "true" religion) and that someday he'll learn the truth. At the very least, I am likely to just decide it isn't important and not think about it at all. All of these are ways to translate the new information so that it fits in my prearranged worldview.

Changing one's worldview is very, very hard. Called "transformation" (to distinguish it from "translation"), it requires no less than a complete tearing down of everything someone thinks is true about themselves and the world. It usually only happens along with traumatic events that provoke existential crises. Why do I exist? What does it mean? What if there is no God? Or if there is, why did He let this horrible thing happen? Outside of traumatic events, it typically only happens when someone is in the Self-Actualization/ Existential stage where they have completed their life's work, are perhaps aging and facing death and ask "now what?"

And yet, this is precisely what must happen in order to reach the sixth Transpersonal stage. People who reach this stage early in life almost always do so through traumatic life events that forced their transformation. But it is only in the sixth stage that Light is found in profusion. Brothers and others who have reached that stage, even fleetingly, seem to shine with a certain wisdom and peace that others seek.

Two-Way Street

Contrary to how we want to think about ourselves, we don't just attain a developmental stage and never lose it. In reality, our mental states change depending on how satisfied a developmental stage's needs are. Called Maslow's Hierarchy of Needs, it states that once a person has a "lower" need mostly fulfilled, only then can he focus on the next "higher" need. Put simply, a person only cares about their safety once they aren't starving, and they only care about fitting in when they feel safe within the group. Further, they only care about succeeding in the group if they are a member of it.

But the hierarchy goes both ways. A very successful business man will no longer care about his public image if a war destroys his house and leaves him starving to death. If you no longer feel safe somewhere, you aren't going to try to impress the neighbors.

And as the hierarchy goes both ways, so do the mental states and capacities that correspond with them. As formally intelligent, kind people move down the hierarchy, their cognition, emotions and behavior will revert to their levels when they first developed them. So that person who is intelligent and kind when he is a successful member of society will become more selfish and childish as he loses esteem, is kicked out of his group, fears for his life, and struggles to survive. This is why when people are so deeply frightened and traumatized, they have trouble speaking. They return to their preverbal selves. This is also why during natural disasters many people revert to the "me and mine" mental state of a two-year-old where it is okay to push and shove, loot and steal.

Because of the two-way movement of cognition and mental state based on one's hierarchy of needs levels, we essentially "unlearn" everything as our needs become less fulfilled or we feel more threatened. This is how "transformation" happens.

The person, either through traumatic events, existential crisis, or some fearful or stressful situation is brought back to an infantile state of vulnerability and then learns a new language, new concepts, new worldviews, new rules and how they fit within them. They are born anew.

This is the same process used by many groups, but the most perfect example is U.S. military boot camp. A new recruit is brought in and his identity is stripped by hair cutting and standardized uniforms. He is subjected to extreme physical challenges, personally belittled, disrupted in food and sleep, and made vulnerable in a host of other ways (Survival and Safety Stages). Then he is gradually taught the specialized language, information, rules, and requirements of the military. He starts to identify himself as a soldier and part of the team (Belonging Stage), and is encouraged to distinguish himself (Esteem Stage). He has been transformed in a way quite different than if he were just given a book of terms, rules and requirements and asked to learn them.

Likewise religious groups from cults to mainstream churches use the same techniques. These groups look for people in some kind of crisis and feeling lost (Survival Stage). They befriend them and start bringing them to their religious services where they are showered with love and acceptance by strangers (Safety Stage). Eventually, they are asked to come join the group and to attend educational groups (Belonging Stage). As they progress in learning the ideas, rules, behaviors and worldview of the church, they distinguish themselves and are held in esteem by the group (Esteem Stage).

None of this is to belittle any of these groups. On the contrary, all groups engage in these activities. It is how people naturally learn and grow within a group. It also shows us what it takes for someone to truly change and transform, which is why it is important for us to know in bringing Light to our brethren.

Freemasonic Initiation as Transformation

According to anthropologist Van Gennep (1909), initiation is divided into three phases. First is the "pre-liminal" or pre-threshold phase. This is a phase where the individual is either literally or symbolically separated from his previous state. That is, he is removed from everything familiar. The "liminal" or threshold phase comes next and is marked by trials, challenges and things that will disorient him. Lastly, in the post-liminal or post-threshold phase of initiation he is accepted into and integrated into his new group or status therein.

In Freemasonry, the pre-liminal phase is all of the preparations discussed in Chapters 3 and 4. These include the entire application, information and investigation process. Seldom do we go through such a process, especially one that is both so in depth and yet retains so many secret and mysteries. Then when he is picked up and driven to the lodge by a brother, changed into unfamiliar clothes, and left in the preparation room, he is definitely outside of the familiar.

The post-liminal initiation phase in Masonic ritual includes the post initiation lectures and instruction as well as the very important mentorship that will be discussed in the next chapter.

Having laid the groundwork on how human cognition develops and is altered, we will now concentrate on how Freemasonic initiations use that liminal phase to make the candidate susceptible to transformation.

The key to an effective initiation is to move the candidate down the hierarchy of needs. This is done through disorientation, vulnerability and fear. If properly and solemnly prepared, the candidate should be a bit nervous and thus, in a heightened state of awareness. He is in a strange place and unfamiliar with the norms and rules of the group. He is already reduced to the early Belonging Stage. The use of blindfolds, binding cords, and disorientation due to repeated circumambulations make him highly vulnerable. When physical challenges (minor in the first two degrees but significant in the third) and seemingly potential death are also introduced – if they are done with seriousness, focus, and intention – the candidate will have passed back through Safety Stage and have serious concerns about his survival (Survival Stage). It is at this stage when his mind is as open as a young child's, that he is exposed to a variety of symbols, words and concepts that are central to the Masonic myth.

He does of course survive and is symbolically reborn. Upon being reborn, he is assured of his safety by the Worshipful Master in the Five Points of Fellowship. He is welcomed a member and over the ensuing lectures and his mentorship, he should become deeply inculcated with the culture of our fraternity. This includes our specialized jargon (i.e. "cowan") and the unique cadence of Masonic ritual, the ethical and moral lessons of our Work, the symbols and emblems, tenets and principles, and social conventions of lodge and brotherhood. As he improves in Masonic knowledge and begins the performance of his obligations, he is assured of 'public and private esteem."

If the initiatic work is done slipshod, with sideline chatter and ruffians who giggle and joke, then our new brother will end just feeling like he went through a strange ritual to join a club of guys from town. But if the ritual was done with solemnity and seriousness, each officer with intent focus on the importance of his part, the brother will feel like something has changed in him and that he is now part of something larger and greater than he is by himself. He will begin to see the world differently and will gradually change his behaviors to conform to his obligation and the tenets and principles of the fraternity. He will truly have initiated a new beginning.

Chapter 7: Mentorship

The greatest good you can do for another is not just to share your riches but to reveal to him his own.
– Benjamin Disraeli

As discussed in the previous chapter, mentorship is critical to an effective "post-liminal" integration of the new brother into the lodge, the fraternity, and the cognitive worldview change that constitutes Masonic Light. It is only through effective mentorship that the new brother can begin to learn the language and culture of his new self and group identity, making him feel a part of the group – and thus more likely to keep coming – and eventually to develop esteem in the group that will lead him to excel in ritual and lodge leadership.

This mentorship can be performed by a sole appointed person or by a committee. There are distinct advantages to both approaches but I would argue that the committee model, when done effectively, can produce beneficial opportunities that a sole mentor cannot. These will be explored later.

Nonetheless, having at least one mentor is critical to the successful integration of the new member.

Successful integration into the lodge involves three things:
1) The new brother feeling included by the group
2) The new brother having something to do
3) The new brother having something to learn

This requires work on the part of both the mentor(s) and the new brother. And let's be frank, new behaviors aren't learned over night. It takes time and energy to create a new habit; a new pattern in your life. That is what we ought to be demanding of our new brothers: that they create a new pattern where lodge activities are priorities and Masonic Light actually is the rule and guide to their conduct. Thus, we cannot expect the mentorship to completed in one or two months. The mentorship should be at least a one-year formal process.

Mentoring Committee's Responsibilities

The mentoring committee should be a team of at least three brothers, with at least one being a Past Master. Ideally, at least one of the team members should be fairly new to the fraternity so that they still remember how intimidating and challenging being a new brother can be. They will remember all of the times when they weren't told things that turned out awkward or embarrassing, and they will be sure not to let this happen to their new brothers. In fact, being on the mentorship committee should be required of all new brothers during their year of mentorship. This will give them an official role that will keep them invested and involved plus; the best way to learn something is to have to teach it.

The committee should assign one "point person" to be the new brother's primary mentor and contact person, and the rest will serve as support and back up to the primary mentor.

The mentoring job begins at the moment that the candidate is voted on and accepted for initiation. Jobs to perform before the candidate is initiated include:
- assist in conveying congratulations of the affirmative vote, and firm up contact information including email address and other preferred methods of communication.
- inform the candidate of the number, and a rough schedule, of the degrees ahead
- coordinate degree schedule between body head and candidate for all upcoming degrees
- inform candidate of the expected length, and a very superficial summary, of the upcoming degrees
- prepare candidate for any specific knowledge (e.g. signs) which would be required of the candidate in the degrees
- pick up and accompany the candidate to required initiation
- introduce the candidate to assembled brethren and show him around the building (at the very least, show him the location of the bathroom)

After the degree, the mentor is required to:
- conduct ongoing, post-degree summarization of the significance of degrees just taken in follow up conversations with new brother
- mentor the new brother in degree proficiencies
- make sure he is prepared with any signs, salutes, words that he will be asked in the upcoming degree (if any)

Once he has been admitted, the mentor should make sure that each of these happen:

- review with the new brother lodge and ritual protocols (meaning of knocks, signs, salutes, manner of address, Masonic phrases)
- supervise the new brother's performance in lodge (e.g. signs, salutes)
- oversee new brother's proper attire and conduct in lodge
- quiz, invite questions, and otherwise engage the new brother's observations of ritual and floorwork observed at each regular meeting and degree conferral
- inform the new brother of the significance and expectations of the various chairs and mentor him in readiness and selection for offices of the bodies
- introduce him to each current officer and other members of the mentorship committee so that he know who to talk to about various issues
- explain to him the workings of the whole Masonic family (DeMolay, Rainbow, Eastern Star, York and Scottish Rite)
- explain how to get involved in lodge activities
  - o assign him a piece of ritual to learn, especially in the opening or closing
  - o put him on an active committee. Good committees to put him on (even if the lodge has to create such a committee) would be: Mentoring committee (to help integrate new members), Education committee (to organize and lead Masonic education for each meeting), Social committee (to organize monthly fraternal gatherings), and Community committees (to get the members involved *as members* in public events and good works).

- remind and personally invite the new brother, by direct communication, of all upcoming meetings, lodge social events or of any non-home-based activities which may be of interest
- make sure that the new brother is personally greeted at each meeting
- directly account to Worshipful Master the brother's attendance at all regularly called assemblies

If we do these things, then the new brother will develop through the Membership and Self-Esteem stages and become fully integrated and invested into our beloved fraternity. Instead of phantom members who receive the degrees and never return, we will have cultivated the very type of man that we seek to have in our ranks – informed, engaged and active.

The Three Virtues

Charcoal illustration by Lee Woodward Zeigler. Original size: 17.2 cm X 14 cm. Reprinted from a plate inserted after page 2000 of *The History of Freemasonry, Its Legends and Traditions, Its Chronological History,* by Albert Gallatin Mackey. Published by The Masonic History Company, New York and London: 1906. Volume Seven. [Templar Edition: Number 171 of 750.]

Chapter 8: Daily Freemasonry

Masonry is an art, useful and extensive, which comprehends within its circle every branch of useful knowledge and learning, and stamps an indelible mark of preeminence on its genuine professors, which neither chance, power, nor fortune can bestow.
– William Preston

The lessons of Freemasonry are meant to be lived and not simply learned. All too often we are inspired by some experience and carry away from it a sense that an important change has taken place. Yet, over time we get distracted by the minutia of the daily grind and nothing really does change. Gradually we become like those Sunday morning churchgoers who get inspired before lunch and forget it all by dinner.

In order for Freemasonry to reach its stated goals, it needs to be a daily part of each brother's life. Not just once a month for two hours plus an occasional fundraiser. For real transformation to take place, the lessons of our fraternity need to be reinforced daily by study and practice.

Daily Study

Few other fields are as broad and diverse for study than the field of Freemasonry. There is, of course, learning ritual lines for initiations and holding offices, but there is so much more. Any brother can, if he puts a little effort into it, find something of interest to pursue. A bibliography is provided in the appendices.

For those brothers with an interest in ritual, they can examine our rituals from many different angles besides rote memorization of lines. They can be researched for their history, their dramatic techniques, the symbolism of the floorwork (as the officers move around the lodge their positions form various geometric shapes), their psychological and spiritual effects, how they differ in various cultures and more.

For those brethren interested in history, the sky is the limit. Besides studying the history and evolution of the various rituals and lodges, our ranks have been filled with numerous historical figures: celebrities, athletes, politicians, war heroes, peace activists, authors and artists. Others have studied the various lodge jewels and banners, Masonic postcards and stamps, and all of the other tools and trinkets used by the fraternity through history. The topics for study are limited only by the student's imagination.

Some brothers are interested in Masonic symbolism. Obvious areas of study are the trestleboards and lodge architecture.

Each component of the ritual, the officer's stations and movements, the lodge furniture and layout are layered with levels of symbolism. For centuries brothers have explored and conjectured about them and there is always room for more; as stated earlier, the revelations are individual and personal. What one brother may find may not be what another brother finds. That is part of the mystery.

Lastly, there is always the esoteric roots of Freemasonry to study. As discussed in Chapter 6, the writers of much of our ritual were convinced that Freemasonry was a descendent of the ancient mystery schools. Thus, they purposefully built into our fraternity symbols and concepts from Hermeticism and the Kabbalah. Each of these areas is a lifelong study unto itself, and progress made in either leads to deeper insights into our own fraternity.

Brothers new and old should be encouraged to engage in some bit of daily study about Masonry. There are lodges of research dedicated solely for this kind of activity, but there are also some regular lodges that focus on education as well. Some of them require each recipient of a degree to write an independent research paper before advancement, and all other members to submit one annually. Receipt of papers and organizing their presentation could be the job of a lodge's Education Committee; a good place for new brothers to get involved.

Practice

There are generally three ways in which people learn: visually, audibly and tactilely. That is, by seeing, by hearing or touching. Each person has one way that works best for him and one that isn't really his style. That is why some kids excel in the classroom where it is reading and writing while others do better in the hands-on trades. Study is great for people who learn visually or audibly. For those who have to feel their Masonry – either physically or emotionally – practice is their method, and there are at least three types of ways to practice Freemasonry daily: prayer, creativity and service.

Prayer

Our rituals are full of beautiful prayers and soliloquies perfectly designed for meditation and reflection. Brothers should consider creating a small altar space in a private corner of their homes dedicated to their Masonic study and prayer. It can be as simple as a small end table with three candles in a triangular pattern and a chair, or as elaborate as a "home lodge" or chamber of reflection with as many of the props and tools as the brother desires and space allows. The point is to have a place of solitude where he can offer up his daily devotions to Deity and reinforce his commitment to uphold and live our Masonic tenets and virtues.

Creativity

Many people learn best when they can literally put their hands on something. For these brothers it could be very useful for them to actually make things. There is a different level of understanding one gets if they actually carve a small set of each order of architecture, use a plumb and level, or carve a block of granite out of rough stone. Or if one makes a full model (life size or smaller) of the layout of the lodge complete with all of the symbolic features such as the three support pillars, the clouded canopy and the lodge ornaments. They could paint new trestleboards, build models of the Kabbalistic Tree of Life... again, the options are limited only by the brother's interests and imagination.

Both ancient and modern practitioners of alchemy speak of how the outcome of one's alchemical operation is in part a reflection of their inner, spiritual state. If they are calm, focused and balanced in their minds and hearts, the outcome will be the ideal expected. If they are distracted, emotionally disturbed and unfocused, the outcome will be inferior. Brothers who make things as part of their spiritual study can use this technique as an objective measure of their spiritual (and thus subjective) development.

Service

Many cultures have recommended the practice of living one's spiritual practice through service to others. This is, of course, our tenet of Relief and something we take vows to perform. It is defined in the Masonic Monitor as:

> To relieve the distressed is the duty incumbent on all men, but particularly on Masons, who are linked together by an indissoluble chain of sincere affection. To soothe the unhappy, to sympathize with their misfortunes; to compassionate their miseries; and to restore peace to their troubled minds, is the grand aim we have in view. On this basis we form our friendships and establish our connections.

Lodges regularly do hospital visits for their ailing brethren, help widows with chores such as winterizing their homes, and raise money for good causes. However, rather than doing these sporadically, or on an "as-needed" basis, our brothers could engage it as a daily practice. Such a practice might involve a daily proactive check-in with the widows and older brothers of the lodge. Calling or stopping by to chat with one or two a day, bringing them small items (flowers, fresh bread), asking them if they need anything and generally just making certain that they are okay.

Of course, daily service doesn't have to be limited to within the fraternity. The Masonic Monitor also reads:

> By the exercise of Brotherly Love we are taught to regard the whole human species as one family – the high, the low, the rich, the poor – who, created by one Almighty Parent, and inhabitants of the same planet, are to aid, support and protect each other.

Thus, brothers who choose to practice service as their daily Freemasonry could find ways to aid and support their entire communities. The possibilities for service are as endless as are the instances of human suffering, big and small, in the world.

Just for a moment, imagine if every single member of a lodge made it a regular practice to do one of these types of daily Freemasonry. If every member was either studying, praying, creating or serving. Even a small lodge of twenty men could make a huge impact on their lodge and their communities. Five brothers actively researching and doing presentations to the lodge. How everyone's education would bloom! Five brothers praying daily and deepening their connection to our tenets, principles and the Divine. How beneficial such wise men would be! Five brothers creating or recreating items from Masonic history and symbolism and discussing their findings as they do so. The insights that would be gained! And lastly, if five brothers reached out every day in service to one other brother, widow or community member in need. In a week they would have provided relief to 35 people and in a month to 150. Imagine the suffering they could ease and the good they could do. And what better way is there to ensure that the world at large continues convinced of our good effects? We would make a visible, positive change in our communities and men who want to do likewise –the exact kind of men we want to attract – would come knocking at our doors.

A Lodge for the Reception of a Fellow Craft

EMBLEMATIC STRUCTURE OF FREEMASONRY

RED CROSS CONSTANTINE

ACTIVE 33°

ROYAL ORDER SCOTLAND

COUNCIL S.J. 19° TO 30°

SUBLIME PRINCE OF THE ROYAL SECRET

S.J. CONSISTORY 31—32

HONORARY 33°

A.A.O.N.M.S. SHRINE

KNIGHT COMMANDER OF THE COURT OF HONOR

YORK RITE

SCOTTISH RITE

CONFERRED BY COMMANDERY
ORDER OF KNIGHTS TEMPLAR COMMANDERY
ORDER OF KNIGHTS OF MALTA
ORDER OF THE RED CROSS

CONFERRED BY COUNCIL
SUPER EXCELLENT MASTER COUNCIL
SELECT MASTER
ROYAL MASTER

CONFERRED BY CHAPTER
MARK MASTER
MOST EXCELLENT MASTER
PAST MASTER (VIRTUAL)
ROYAL ARCH MASON CHAPTER

32	
31	GRAND INSPECTOR INQUISITOR COMMANDER
30	KNIGHT OF KADOSH
29	KNIGHT OF ST. ANDREW
28	KNIGHT OF THE SUN
27	KNIGHT COMMANDER OF THE TEMPLE
26	PRINCE OF MERCY
25	KNIGHT OF THE BRAZEN SERPENT
24	PRINCE OF THE TABERNACLE
23	CHIEF OF THE TABERNACLE
22	KNIGHT OF THE ROYAL AXE
21	NOACHITE OR PRUSSIAN KNIGHT
20	MASTER AD VITAM
19	GRAND PONTIFF
18	KNIGHT OF THE ROSE CROIX
17	KNIGHTS OF THE EAST & WEST
16	PRINCE OF JERUSALEM
15	KNIGHT OF THE EAST OR SWORD
14	GRAND ELECT MASON
13	MASTER OF THE NINTH ARCH
12	GRAND MASTER ARCHITECT
11	SUBLIME MASTER ELECTED
10	MASTER ELECT OF FIFTEEN
9	MASTER ELECT OF NINE
8	INTENDANT OF THE BUILDING
7	PROVOST & JUDGE
6	INTIMATE SECRETARY
5	PERFECT MASTER
4	SECRET MASTER

CONSISTORY OF PRINCES OF THE ROYAL SECRET
19° TO 32° CHIVALRIC

COUNCIL CHAPTER
15° 15° 17° TO 18° HISTORIC RELIGIOUS

LODGE OF PERFECTION
4° TO 14° INEFFABLE DEGREES

CHAPTER S.A.
15° TO 18°

4°—14° S.J.

BLUE G LODGE
MASTER MASON

FELLOW G CRAFT

ENTERED G APPRENTICE

EASTERN STAR

Chapter 9: Further Light

Perfect truth is not attainable anywhere. We style this Degree that of Perfection; and yet what it teaches is imperfect and defective. Yet we are not to relax in the pursuit of truth, nor contentedly acquiesce in error. It is our duty always to press forward in the search; for though absolute truth is unattainable, yet the amount of error in our views is capable of progressive and perpetual diminution; and thus Masonry is a continual struggle toward the light.
– Albert Pike

There is an endless supply of Light provided by reception of the symbolic degrees and regular study of our Masonic rituals, emblems and symbols. Esteemed brothers down the through the ages have devoted entire lifetimes and never drained the well of wisdom contained there.

And yet, all Light we receive is colored by the lens through which we view it. Just as Divine Truth shines through from all religions, no matter how diverse, Masonic Light shines through in different ways in its various rites and allied degrees. The Light is ultimately the same but each body changes the hue of the Light so that it emphasizes and expands on different lessons and insights. For this reason, some brothers might be interested in and benefit from the initiations and lessons of other Masonic bodies. The major sources of further Light in Masonry are the Scottish Rite, the York Rite and a number of "allied" degrees.

Scottish Rite Masonry

The Scottish Rite is one of the appendant bodies of Freemasonry that a Master Mason may join for further exposure to the principles of Freemasonry. Building upon the teachings of the symbolic degrees, Scottish Rite provides further moral and ethical education through twenty-nine degrees performed in the manner of dramatic presentations. These teachings can be very beautiful, moving and profound and are recommended for all brothers seeking to contemplate these topics. However, these rituals are not initiatic as we have defined that term. The candidates watch a morality play but are not truly active participants. There is no equivalent to the liminal states and development stage transitions that are experienced in the Symbolic degrees. Scottish Rite rituals are instructive but not transformative.

York Rite Masonry

The York Rite is another appendant body of Freemasonry that a Master Mason may join for further Light. Also building upon the teachings of the symbolic degrees, York Rite completes and expands on the Divine Truth explored in Blue Lodge. That which was lost is found in the fourth degree of Royal Arch Masonry.

The York Rite itself is more of a collection of separate Masonic bodies rather one unified body such as Scottish Rite. It is comprised of three bodies:
- Chapter of Royal Arch Masons which confers four degrees
- Council of Royal and Select Masters also known as the Council of Cryptic Masons which confers two degrees
- Order of the Knights Templar which confers four degrees

The degrees of the York Rite are extremely powerful and moving, filled with layers of symbolism and meaning. They are also true initiations with full participation of the candidates, utilizing trials and challenges to effect cognitive change, and, if done well, resulting in a transformative experience.

While neither the York Rite or the Scottish Rite are essential to a Mason's quest for further Light, both are well established ritual systems already in place for ease of access. More importantly, they can be excellent networks of like-minded brothers seeking more out of their Masonry than business meetings and dinners.

Allied Bodies

In addition to the York and Scottish Rites, there are a number of other appendant and allied Masonic bodies focusing on various other aspects of Freemasonry – cultural, practical, research and esoteric. Some of them require membership in either York or
Scottish Rite beforehand. Some are open to all Master Masons. Many of them are invitational only. Some of the invitational orders are even required to reject any application if the brother asked to join. However, a brother can express interest *without asking to join* and this will often result in an invitation.

Below are descriptions taken from the web pages of several of the largest and most respected bodies. Further information can be found at: http://www.yorkrite.com/Honorlinks.htm

The Worshipful Society of Free Masons, Rough Masons, Wallers, Slaters, Paviors, Plaisterers and Bricklayers

This Masonic Society exists to perpetuate a memorial of the practices of operative
Free Masons existing prior to modern speculative Freemasonry. Membership of the Society is restricted to those who are Master Masons, Mark Master Masons and Holy Royal Arch Companions in good standing.

Societas Rosicruciana in Civitatibus Foederatis (SRICF)

The objects of the SRICF are:

1. To afford mutual aid and encouragement in working out the great problems of Life; and in searching out the secrets of Nature; to facilitate the study of the system of Philosophy founded upon the Kabbalah and the doctrine of Hermes Trismegistus, which was inculcated by the original Fratres Rosae Crucis, in A.D.1450; and to investigate the meaning and symbolism of all that now remains of the wisdom, art and literature of the ancient world.

2. To consider and examine the philosophy, iconology, and literature of Freemasonry, to gain a deeper understanding of History, Mythology, Legend, Symbolism, and Science in the study of Freemasonry;

3. To establish a common bond and draw within our ranks men of scientific inclination, students of philosophy, science, and religion, and those interested therein; and

4. To promote the study of science, religion, and philosophy, and the histories thereof, to the end that our Fraters, and those within their influence, may be enlightened by their efforts.

Membership is by invitation only and predicated on regular mainstream Masonic affiliation as well as a profession of Christian faith.

Grand College of Rites

The Grand College of Rites is a "regular" Masonic body, dedicated to preserving the history and rituals of defunct and inactive Masonic orders. In particular, it has for its major objects:

5. The study of the history and ritual of all Rites, Systems and Orders of Freemasonry not under the control, jurisdiction and/or stewardship or regularly existing and recognized Masonic bodies.

6. The elimination of sporadic efforts to resuscitate or perpetuate Rites, Systems and Orders of Freemasonry in the United States, except to bring them under control of the Grand College of Rites.

7. The collection and preservation of rituals of various Rites, Systems and Orders of Freemasonry ordinarily not available to Masonic students.

Any Master Mason holding membership and in good standing in a regular symbolic Lodge recognized by a majority of the Grand Lodges of Freemasonry in the United States may petition for membership in the Grand College of Rites.

Knight Masons (KM)

The Grand Council of Knight Masons of the United States of America, in consideration of its origin strives to:

1. Perpetuate the ancient rituals of the Irish Masonic Canon, (the "Green" degrees) by promoting their frequent and regular conferral in its constituent councils, and by its expectation that such conferral will be executed with an accuracy, a precision, and a dramatic power congruent with the highest traditions of the Masonic institution.

2. Elevate to membership in its constituent councils only those Freemasons who in their character and persons have amply and thoroughly demonstrated in their Masonic lives, by means of a faithful attachment to the institution, a true and honorable record of service to its goals, and a genuine dedication to its high ideals.

3. Foster in its constituent councils the regular exploration and study of the Masonic Tradition and Heritage by means of an aggressive program of scholarly inquiry and research, and to pursue that Masonic learning in the spirit of our Celtic forbears who kept the light of faith burning in times of darkness.

4. Encourage its constituent councils to discover in the pleasures and diversions of the festive board that warm fellowship and that joyous fraternity, which have ever characterized and actuated the great spirit of this Ancient Craft.

5. Promote the charitable dimension so central to, and inherent in, Masonic life and tradition by obliging its constituent councils to contribute with customary Masonic liberality to those institutions,

both Masonic and non-Masonic, which serve the needs of the greater community.

Allied Masonic Degrees (AMD)

The Allied Masonic Degrees are an invitational organization, and requires membership in the Royal Arch as well as the Symbolic Lodge.

The Allied Masonic Degrees are detached degrees some of which, many years ago, were conferred under Craft warrants and formed part of the then loosely governed Freemasonry of the period.

Many of these detached degrees became dormant in some places, although in others they were conferred as side degrees. In time, the better of these degrees were grouped together in an organized body under the title of Allied Masonic Degrees. The degrees comprising the system in our Jurisdiction in the U.S.A. are the Royal Ark Mariner, Secret Monitor, Knight of Constantinople, Saint Lawrence the Martyr, Architect, Superintendent, Grand Tilers of Solomon, Master of Tyre, Excellent Master, Installed Sovereign Master, Installed Commander Noah, Red Branch of Eri and Ye Ancient Order of Corks. They are conferred in the United States in Councils chartered by the Grand Council. Each Council is limited to twenty-seven members, with two exceptions. One of these Councils is known as the Council of the Nine Muses and is limited to nine members. The other is Grand Masters Council, which has what is known as a roving charter. The purpose of the latter Council is to provide a place of membership in the Allied Masonic Degrees for brethren residing in localities where Councils have not been organized. Membership in every Council of Allied Masonic Degrees is by invitation, and is predicated on membership in the Royal Arch Chapter.

In addition to perpetuating these degrees, there is still another and equally important purpose. It is to bring together, in small groups, Freemasons who are interested in the advancement of all Masonry, preparing themselves to better serve the Craft through the medium of study and research. By limiting the membership in a Council and securing membership only by invitation, the result is a congenial group able to enjoy full fellowship when meeting together. Wherever there is an active Council of Allied Masonic Degrees, it exerts an influence for the betterment of Freemasonry in all the Masonic Bodies.

There is no intention on the part of the Allied Masonic Degrees to detract from any organized and established body of Masonry. On the contrary, you will find our members active, beyond the average, in all local Masonic bodies. The real purpose is to stimulate interest in Masonry in general and bring together in small groups those who are interested in the study of Masonic subjects. Thus they are better enabled to serve the Craft.

Red Cross of Constantine (RCC)

The Red Cross of Constantine is officially The Masonic and Military Order of the Red Cross of Constantine and the Orders of the Holy Sepulchre and St. John the Evangelist, the latter two of which are called the Appendant Orders. There are also two chair degrees conferred on the Viceroy and Sovereign of a Conclave, and two honorary orders: Knight Commander of Constantine and Knight Grand Cross.

The purpose of the Constantinian Orders are to commemorate the first elevation of Christianity from the position of a despised and proscribed heresy to that of a legally recognized and honored religion, to cultivate the social virtues, appeal to the intellectual and moral qualities, preserve as far as possible the customs of the fraternity and bring about good fellowship and understanding between all branches of Masonry.

Knights Companions of the Order meet in Conclaves of the Red Cross of Constantine, and a member must be a Royal Arch Mason in good standing and subscribe to a belief in the Christian religion as revealed in the New Testament. Membership is by invitation and each Conclave has a prescribed membership limit.

Royal Order of Scotland (ROOS)

Originally, membership in the Order was limited to Scotsmen or those of Scottish descent, but latter the privilege was extended to Master Masons of other nationalities. The Order is not conferred on anyone who has not received the 32nd-degree of the Ancient and Accepted Scottish Rite, except by waiver from the Provincial Grand Master.

The Order is one which is, from its historical associations, peculiarly interesting to Scottsmen, and each year on the 4th of July (old style), the anniversary of the day on which the Battle of Bannockburn was fought, the Grand Lodge of the Order, as well as some of the Provincial Grand Lodges, continue the ancient custom of the Order by holding a festival, at which the Toast to the Immortal Memory of King Robert the Bruce, the hero of Bannockburn and Restorer of the Order is proposed in an oration by one of the Brethren, and honoured in silence. The Degrees of the Order are most beautiful and impressive, and inculcate the three great principles of Freemasonry — Brotherly Love, Relief and Truth.

The Royal Order comprises two Degrees, that of Heredom of Kilwinning and that of the Rosy Cross. Tradition tells us that the former was established in Judea, in Palestine, but whether at the time of the Crusaders of much earlier origin, tradition is silent.

The word "Heredom" has been variously interpreted, but the most obvious derivation is from the Hebrew word "Harodim", meaning "The Rulers", and the name of Kilwinning refers to the re-establishment of the Order by King Robert the Bruce at Kilwinning, where he presided as its first Grand Master.

The Degree of Heredom of Kilwinning is a peculiarly interesting Degree and full of instruction to Craft Masons, as in its lectures it explains the symbolism and teaching contained in the first three Degrees of what is sometimes referred to as St. John s Masonry.

The Rosy Cross Degree tradition takes its origin on the field of Bannockburn, on Summer St. John's Day 1314, and was instituted by King Robert the Bruce, who having in the course of the battle for Scottish independence, received assistance from a body of sixty-three knights who may have been original Knights Templar and Freemasons. He conferred upon them as a reward for their services the civil rank of Knighthood. Each received a characteristic considered descriptive of his performance at Bannockburn. He granted them permission to confer the honor on such Scottish Freemasons professing the Christian religion as had shown themselves worthy of the honor. This degree, as its name implies, deals more with the subject matter of the Rose Croix Degree of the Ancient and Accepted Scottish Rite than with that of Craft Masonry.

Epilogue

On May 21, 1772, William Preston gave the following oration at the occasion of the first demonstration before the Grand Master (Moderns) of Preston's degree system:

> If the privileges of masonry are so valuable, as to intitle their possessors to respect and esteem, by promoting virtue and rewarding merit; why are not their good effects more conspicuous, and why are they not publicly exposed for the general advantage of mankind? If our privileges were common, and indiscriminately bestowed, the design of the institution would not only be subverted, but being familiar, like some other important matters, it would lose its value, and sink into disregard. It is a weakness in human nature, that men are generally more charmed with novelty, than the real worth or intrinsic value of things. This is not confined to masonry; even the operations of nature, though beautiful, magnificent and useful, are overlooked because common and

familiar. The sun rises and sets, the sea flows and reflows, rivers glide along their channels, trees and plants vegetate, men and beasts act, and all these, ever present to our eyes, yet remain unnoticed, and excite not one single emotion, either in admiration of the great cause, or of gratitude for the blessings conferred. Even virtue itself is not exempted from this unhappy bias in the constitution of mankind. Novelty influences all our actions, all our determinations. Every thing that is new or difficult in the acquisition, however trifling or insignificant, readily captivates the imagination and ensures a temporary admiration; while what is familiar, or easily attained, however noble, or eminent for utility, is sure to be disregarded by the giddy and the unthinking.

It is a truth too obvious to be concealed, that the privileges of masonry have been too common. Hence we may assign a reason why their good effects are not more conspicuous. Several persons enroll their names in our records merely to oblige their friends; and reflect not on the consequences of such a measure, nor enquire into the nature of their particular engagements. Not a few are prompted by motives of interest; and many are introduced with no better view than to please as good companions. A general odium, or at least a careless indifference, is the result of such conduct. But here the evil stops not. These persons, ignorant of our noble principles, probably without any real defect in their own morals, are led to recommend others of the same cast with themselves for the same purpose. Thus, behold the end! The most sacred part of masonry is turned into scoff and ridicule, and the superficial practices of a luxurious age bury in oblivion principles which have dignified princes and the most exalted characters.

Many have been deluded by the vague supposition that the mysteries of masonry were merely nominal, that the practices established among us were slight and superficial, and that our ceremonies were of such trifling import, as to be adopted or waved at pleasure. Having passed through the useful formalities, they have accepted offices, and assumed the government of Lodges, equally unacquainted with the duties of the trusts reposed in them, and the design of the society they pretended to govern. The consequence is obvious; anarchy and confusion ensue, and the substance is lost in the shadow. Thus men eminent for ability, for rank and fortune, view with indifference the distinguished honours of masonry, and either accept offices with reluctance, or reject them with disdain.

Such are the disadvantages under which masonry has long laboured. Every zealous friend to the society must earnestly wish for a reformation of these abuses.

Sadly, much of what Brother Preston wrote 240 years ago still applies. These "disadvantages" have lcd our beloved fraternity to wane in number and good effect over the last several decades. But the tide is turning – a new wave of intelligent young men are seeking once again to dig deeply into the shadows of oblivion for the "substance" upon which Freemasonry was founded.

By understanding the underlying mechanism originally used by Masonry to transform and bring to Light its members, we can once again hope to live up to the words of the Duke of Sussex:

> Masonry is one of the most sublime and perfect institutions that ever was formed for the advancement of happiness, and the general good of mankind, creating, in all its varieties, universal benevolence and brotherly love.

So mote it be.

Bibliography

Churton, Tobias. The Golden Builders: Alchemists, Rosicrucians, and the First Freemasons. New York, NY: Barnes & Noble Publishing, 2002.

Dyer, Colin. William Preston and His Work. London: Lewis Masonic, 1987.

Eliade, Mircea. Rites and Symbols of Initiation. London: Harvill Press, 1958.

Godwin, Joscelyn. Robert Fludd: Hermetic Philosopher and Surveyor of Two Worlds. London: Thames and Hudson, 1979.

Greer, John Michael. Inside a Magical Lodge: Group Ritual in the Western Tradition. St. Paul, MN: Llewellyn Publications, 1998.

Hall, Manley P. The Secret Teachings of All Ages. Los Angeles, CA: The Philosophical Research Society, 1978.

Hammer, Andrew. Observing the Craft: The Pursuit of Excellence in Masonic Labour and Observance. Alexandria, VA: Mindhive Books, 2010.

Hunter, C. Bruce. "Freemasonry and the Mystery Religions," first published in The Plumbline, Winter 2006, via The Ashlar, Issue 30, pp. 38-42

James, William. The Varieties of Religious Experience
(1902). New York, NY: Cosimo Classics, 2007.

Mackey, Albert. Encyclopedia of Freemasonry and Kindred
Sciences. New York, NY:
The Masonic History Company, 1929.

MacNulty, W. Kirk. "A Philosophical Background to
Masonic Symbolism", Heredom Journal of the Scottish Rite
Research Society, Vol. 5, 1996.

MacNulty, W. Kirk. "The Application of Psychology to
Masonic Symbolism" (Appendix II , Freemasonry for Bo-
bos", Heredom Journal of the Scottish Rite Research Society,
Vol. 13, 2005.

Maslow, Abraham. Toward a Psychology of
Being. Princeton, NJ: D. Van Nostrand, 1962.

Ozaniec, Naomi. The Aquarian Qabalah: A Contemporary
Initiation into a Secret Tradition. London: Watkins
Publishing, 2003.

Paden, William. Religious Worlds: the Comparative Study of
Religion, 2nd ed. Boston, MA: Beacon Press, 1994.

Pike, Albert. Morals and Dogma. Charleston, SC: Supreme
Council of the Thirty Third Degree or the Southern
Jurisdiction of the United States 1871.

Ponce, Charles. Kabbalah: An Introduction and Illumination
for the World Today. San Francisco, CA: Straight Arrow
Books, 1973.

Soul of a Second Skin

Can a Christian be kinky? That's a question that is rarely asked. More specifically, can a gay leathermen be a Christian? That is the key question that this book seeks to answer. Nationally known and respected leatherman, author and speaker Hardy Haberman reveals his spiritual journey and gives readers both kinky and straight insight into the soul of his beliefs. His views on the BDSM lifestyle and Christianity are enlightening, entertaining and sometimes controversial, but the story of his journey is sure to be thought provoking.

For anyone seeking to reconcile their religious and spiritual beliefs with their sexuality and kink, this book is a valuable resource. For people unfamiliar with the Leather/BDSM/Fetish community, this book offers a glimpse into the world of radical sexuality. For Christians, it is witness to the extravagant grace of God and a testament to an unconventional pathway to abundant life.

Yes, it is not only possible to be a gay Christian leatherman, but it can be an interesting journey getting there.

Porter, Cliff. The Secret Psychology of Freemasonry. Denver, CO: Starr Publishing, 2011.

Schopenhauer, Arthur. The World as Will and Representation (Die Welt als Wille und Vorstellung), 2nd ed., New York, NY: Dover Publications, 1966.

Stavish, Mark. "The Chamber of Reflection, 2002. http://www.hermeticinstitute.org/docs/chamber.pdf

Taylor, Thomas. Eleusinian and Bacchic Mysteries. Lighting Source Publishers, 1997.

Thomas, J.E. Essay on "The Inner Truths", South Africa, 1896.

Van Gennep, Arnold. The Rites of Passage (1909). Chicago, IL: University of Chicago Press, 1960.

Waite, Arthur E. A New Encyclopedia of Freemasonry (Combined Edition). New York, NY: Weathervane Books, 1970.

Walker, Michael W. "Freemasonry in society – today and tomorrow. Some personal musings." http://freemasonry.bcy.ca/texts/walker.html

Wilber, Ken. Integral Spirituality: A Startling New Role for Religion in the Modern and Postmodern World. Boston, MA: Integral Books, 2006.

Wilber, Ken. The Atman Project: A Transpersonal View of Human Development. Wheaton, IL: The Theosophical Publishing House, 1980.

Wilber, Ken. Up From Eden: A Transpersonal View of Human Evolution. Garden City, NY: Anchor Press/ Doubleday, 1981.

Wilmshurst, W.L. The Meaning of Masonry, by London: William Rider & Son, 1922.

Wood, Douglas & Dimitar, Mavrov. Into Masonic Light. Alexandria, VA: Sheridan Books, 2010.

Acknowledgments

The list of mentor responsibilities were largely the work of Brother Jonathan Park and was used by permission.

The Petitioner's Questionnaire was modified from that of Phoenix Lodge #105, Grand Lodge of New Hampshire and was used by permission.

Large parts of the "Expectations of the Lodge", in particular the portions on time and money commitments, were taken from "Commitment for Freemasonry" published by the Grand Lodge of Australia.

All of the images in this book, except the pyramid of Maslow's Hierarchy of Needs created by the author, are in the public domain and are stored in the resource archives of the Grand Lodge of British Columbia and the Yukon. They can be found at: www.freemasonry.bcy.ca

Summary of Freemasonic Informational Meeting

<u>The Goals and Principles of Freemasonry</u>

The short answer is that Freemasonry provides a forum and mechanism to promote in its members:
- moral and mental education
- spiritual growth and enlightenment
- fraternal bonding

And that such enlightened men, when banded together, will naturally seek to promote a more moral and harmonious society founded on the principles of equality/ brotherly love, charity, and Divine Truth and supported by the virtues of temperance, fortitude, prudence and justice.

A longer version is the Declaration of Principles (Vermont version provided). It reads:

FREEMASONRY is a charitable, benevolent, educational and religious society. Its principles are proclaimed as widely as men will hear. Its only secrets are in its methods of recognition and of symbolic instruction.

IT IS CHARITABLE in that it is not organized for profit and none of its income inures to the benefit of any individual, but all is devoted to the promotion of the welfare and happiness of mankind.

IT IS BENEVOLENT in that it teaches and exemplifies altruism as a duty.

IT IS EDUCATIONAL in that it teaches by prescribed ceremonials a system of morality and brotherhood based upon the Sacred Law.

IT IS RELIGIOUS in that it teaches monotheism, the Volume of the Sacred Law is open upon its altars whenever a Lodge is in session, reverence for God is ever present in its ceremonial, and to its Brethren are constantly addressed lessons of morality; yet it is not sectarian or theological.

IT IS A SOCIAL ORGANIZATION only so far as it furnishes additional inducements that men may foregather in numbers, thereby providing more material for its primary work of education, of worship and of charity.

THROUGH the improvement and strengthening of the character of the individual man, Freemasonry seeks to improve the community. Thus it impresses upon its members the principles of personal righteousness and personal responsibility, enlightens them as to those things which make for human welfare, and inspires them with the feeling of charity, or good will, toward all mankind which will move them to translate principle and conviction into action..

TO THAT END, it teaches and stands for the worship of God; truth and justice; fraternity and philanthropy; and enlightenment and orderly liberty, civil, religious and intellectual. It charges each of its members to be true and loyal to the government of the country to which he owes allegiance and to be obedient to the law of any state in which he may be.

IT BELIEVES that the attainment of the objectives is best accomplished by laying a broad basis of principle upon which men of every race, country, sect and opinion may unite rather than by setting up a restricted platform upon which only those of certain races, creeds and opinions can assemble.

BELIEVING THESE THINGS, this Grand Lodge affirms its continued adherence to that ancient and approved rule of Freemasonry which forbids the discussion in Masonic meetings of creeds, politics, or other topics likely to excite personal animosities.

IT FURTHER AFFIRMS its conviction that it is not only contrary to the fundamental principles of Freemasonry, but dangerous to its unity, strength, usefulness and welfare, for Masonic Bodies to take action or attempt to exercise pressure or influence for or against any legislation, or in any way to attempt to procure the election or appointment of government officials, or to influence them, whether or not members of the Fraternity, in the performance of their official duties. The true Freemason will act in civil life according to his individual judgment and the dictates of his conscience.

The foregoing was adopted by the Grand Lodge of Vermont at its 1940 Annual Communication. Many other American Grand Lodges have adopted the same Declaration. It is a plain statement of the aims, objects and conduct of Freemasonry for *all* to read and understand.

Lodge Activities

Masonic Lodges are busy organizations. Typically we have one "regular meeting" per month. At these meetings there are two types of agenda. The first is like the business meeting of any other organization. It just takes us a bit longer to call the meeting to order because we use a longer opening ritual than most civic clubs do. However, this opening ritual is important for it reminds us of the values and lessons we have learned and committed to in our dealings with our brethren and all of mankind. Once the lodge is "open," we do the usual business stuff of reading minutes, approving reports, paying bills, handling old and new business and planning projects. The second type of agenda is one in which new members are received. This is done with a beautiful ritual, centuries old, which is designed to teach some important lessons and to start the person thinking about his own nature as a spiritual being.

Because of the frequency and importance of our lodge rituals, activities can also include study and practice meetings for lodge officers and others who have ritual roles in various ceremonies. We welcome new faces in many of these roles, so if you are accepted and like this kind of stuff, please let us know.

Education is important in Freemasonry. For that reason, many lodges have monthly Masonic Education nights where brothers can learn more from well-informed brothers about Masonry and share any new discoveries they've made.

Lodges also periodically engage in strictly social events. These can include cookouts, card nights, family movie nights and a whole host of events. Some lodges are more social than others.

Another common lodge activity is fundraising. Because of our charitable works, we often hold raffles, run golf tournaments, have fish fries and other fundraising events. Each member is expected to help in these events to his full capability. Many hands make light work and strengthen our bonds of friendship.

One of our vows is to look after the widows and families of deceased brethren and to aid any sick or distressed brother. Depending on need and circumstances, each brother will be asked to join in these efforts periodically.

To further support our brothers and to strengthen our fraternity, some lodges will organize a visit to a neighboring lodge to witness their degree work or just to reinforce friendships.

Finally, our lodge has occasional obligations to the Grand Lodge, our state organization. There are a few meetings ever year that brothers are strongly encouraged to attend in support of their lodge officers and the Grand Lodge.

Expectations of the Lodge

Membership in a Masonic lodge comes with expectations on the part of the lodge. As a brother, you will be required to meet certain commitments in regards to attendance and time, financial costs, education progress, involvement in lodge functions, and attire and deportment in lodge. Specifically, these are: commitments.

1) Attendance and Time Commitment
   a. To attend lodge meetings, without fail, once per month
   b. If you must miss a meeting, to call the lodge secretary *before* the meeting and inform him as to the reason for your absence
   c. Attend all lodge practices, without fail, when held
   d. Daily study of some aspect of Masonic knowledge
   e. Serve on one or more of the lodge committees. For example, membership, education grounds, hospital visitations, etc.
   f. Attend, several times per year, the social or charitable pursuits of the lodge
   g. Attend the annual Grand Lodge Convocation (once per year) and the annual District Meeting (once per year)

h. Support your lodge in official visitations to other lodges
i. Doing some private visiting to other lodges – perhaps once every two or three months
j. Periodically helping a friend or brother in time of need or distress
k. Occasionally performing some act of kindness for an elderly brother, or for some deceased brother's widow or family
l. Perhaps supporting youth orders attached to Freemasonry

In short, the Masonic life is a pretty full one; both as to commitment of your scarce leisure time, and in your pride and self-satisfaction as to a job done well and faithfully.

2) Financial Commitments
    a. You will have to pay an application fee of $_____ upon joining a lodge.
    b. You will have to pay annual dues of $_____.
    c. You will have to own or buy a dinner suit (and accessories) and possibly a tuxedo (if you become a lodge officer or Grand Officer)
    d. You will be expected to pay for dinners or refreshments before or after lodge.
    e. You will be expected to contribute to lodge charities and fundraisers.
    f. When visiting a lodge, you will be expected to pay for your dinner, buy any raffle tickets and contribute to their charity collection.
    g. You will incur "hidden costs" in:

      i. Driving to lodge meetings and practices
     ii. Driving on lodge visits
   iii. Perhaps taxiing an old or infirm brother to lodge
   iv. Telephone costs

It is obvious that there is a not insignificant (but not overwhelming) monetary outlay required of you. It is suggested to proposed members that this is well worth the cost, as with the necessary enthusiasm, lodge will become a significant part of your life. You will find that is a highly rewarding and financially competitive alternative to other sources of recreation.

3) Educational Progress Commitment
    a. After each degree (of which there are three), you will be required to commit certain portions of information to memory before advancement
    b. If you become an officer, you will be required to perfectly learn your lines and ritual floor work. These are short and simple in lower officers but become substantial as times goes on.
    c. You are highly encouraged to continue your Masonic education by regular reading and study, conversing with well-informed brethren, and possibly pursuing appendant Masonic rites.

4) Involvement Commitment
   a. As noted earlier, you are expected to be involved in all lodge functions, fundraisers, meetings, visitations, good works and other events. Just paying your dues and showing up occasionally is insufficient.

5) Attire and deportment in lodge
   a. As noted earlier, dress codes apply. Freemasonry is important and should be treated as such. Dress as you would for any other important event (e.g. a wedding, business meeting, church).
   b. Behavior during lodge should be respectful, courteous, and friendly but not vulgar or profane.
   c. Behavior during ritual should be solemn and serious.
   d. Behavior after lodge should be cheerful and social without leading to intemperance or excess.
   e. Behavior outside of lodge should reflect the tenets and virtues of our Institution and be of good repute.

What Process to Expect if You Apply for Membership

Now that you have attended the informational meeting, it is recommended that you take some time to reflect on whether or not Freemasonry is right for you at this time. Assess whether the goals and purposes of the fraternity appeal to you. Can you make the significant level of commitment required?

Discuss your interest with your family. Freemasonry is not just a "club." It changes your life forever and works for good in every part of your life. You are joining a new family of brothers who you can rely on but who also expect to be able to rely on you. Is your family okay with you making this level of commitment? Are they willing to be part of it (even if tangentially) as well? To join is a serious commitment with real expectations but to those who fulfill them, the rewards are commensurately great.

If you still want to join, the process goes like this:

1) Complete the application and petitioner questionnaire that you received at the informational meeting.
2) Return both documents to the lodge secretary whose contact information should have been with the application.
3) At the next regular meeting of the lodge, which will be within 30 days from when you apply, your application will be read and an investigation committee formed or activated.
4) The chair of the investigation committee will contact you to set up a date and time for them to come to your house to chat with you and your spouse. This is a fairly informal interview for us to get to know you a little better. This is also a good time for your spouse or family members to ask any questions they may have.
5) At the next regular meeting of the lodge, the committee will report and your petition balloted on.

a. If the vote is in the affirmative, a date for your initiation will be set, and you will be assigned a mentor who will notify you with everything you will need to know in order to be ready. We try to initiate new brothers as soon after acceptance as possible and often can do so in one or two months. But depending on when you apply and other lodge obligations it can potentially take as long as four to six months. If you have any questions, do not hesitate to contact your mentor.

b. If your application is rejected, you will be contacted by the lodge secretary and informed of our regrets.

6) On the night of your initiation, your mentor will pick you up at home and escort you to the lodge. He will also take you home afterward.

7) Your mentor will be your guide as you grow in your Masonic education. Feel free to ask him any questions that come to mind.

Petitioner Questionnaire

Instructions:

In addition to your submission of a petition for the Degrees of Freemasonry, our Lodge requires your completion of this questionnaire to assist us in determining your qualifications for the high standards of Freemasonry.

Petitioners are required to be able to read and write in English as this is an English Speaking Lodge and all our Degree Work is conducted in the English language.

Please read through this whole questionnaire, more especially the certification, before entering any required information. Print in ink or type all answers, all questions MUST BE COMPLETED. If the answer is "none" or "not applicable," state it as such. Do not leave questions blank, misstated, or omit material fact as all statements made by you are subject to verification. If more space is needed, add additional sheets if necessary. The information in this questionnaire will be held as a confidential record for Lodge use only, and will not be shared with or sold to outside agencies. An Investigation Committee of selected Brothers will make contact with you and arrange for an interview prior to the Lodge meeting at which your petition will be reviewed and balloted upon.

1.) Last, First, & Middle Names (*In full and in print*)

2.) Physical Address:

3.) Mailing Address (if different):

4.) Former Names, Aliases, or Nicknames

5.) Email Address(es):

6.) Home Phone Number(s):

7.) Business Phone Number(s):

8.) Cell Phone Number(s):

9.) Are you a Citizen of the United States?   Yes____ No____
(*If no, state your status in the United States and your Country of origin or citizenship*)

10.) Are you of sound physical and mental health? Yes ____
No ____

11.) Are you now, or have you ever been, addicted to the use of intoxicating or habit forming drugs, beverages or chemicals administered legally or not? (*Note: Answering yes to #11 does not automatically exclude you from Membership. If yes, please explain*) Yes____ No____

12.) How long have you lived at your current address?

13.) Where did you previously reside before your current address?

14.) How long did you live at this previous address?

15.) How long have you been a resident of this State?

16.) Are you financially solvent? Yes_____ No_____

17.) What is your Marital Status? _____
Number of Children?_____

18.) Do you live with your family? Yes_____ No_____

19.) How many members live in your household?

20.) How many of them are you financially responsible for?

21.) What is your Spouse's name?

22.) Are you now, or have you ever been, a member of or owed allegiance to any organization, association, movement, group, or combination of persons who advocates the overthrow of the constitutional government of the United States of America by force, violence, or other illegal means, or who seeks to alter the form of government by unconstitutional means? Yes_____ No_____ (*If yes, explain*)

23.) Have you ever been convicted of a felony?
(*Note: Answering yes does not automatically exclude you from Membership. If yes, please explain; if further space is needed, use remarks section.*) Yes _____ No _____

24.) If requested by the Lodge would you be willing to submit, at your own expense, to a criminal background records check with the state? (*Note: Answering no does not automatically exclude you from Membership.*)
Yes_____ No_____

25.) Are you related to anyone connected to this, or any other Masonic Lodge?   Yes____ No____   (*If yes, please list*)
Name   Address   Lodge Name/Number

26.) Did anyone ask you to join the Masonic Fraternity? Yes____ No____
Who?

27.) Are you currently employed? Yes ____ No____

28.) Self Employed? Yes____ No____

29.) Place of Employment?

30.) Business Type?

31.) Your Job Responsibilities?

32.) Please list your employment for the last 3 years. Please include dates, name and address, position, and reason for leaving. (*If additional space is required use additional sheets.*)

33.) Please list the highest level of Education that you have completed. (*High School, GED, College, Graduate School, Trade School, Certificate courses*).

34.) Please list any additional training, licenses, or skills? (*Examples: Commercial Drivers License, EMT, Plumbing, Photograph, Musical, etc.)*

35.) Are you currently, or have you ever been, a member of the United States Military Services? Yes____ No____ Please state Branch and Specialty:

36.) If you answered yes to the previous question, were you honorably discharged? Yes____ No____ (*If no, please explain*)

37.) Are you fully aware that all organizations, Masonic Lodges included, must have financial income to meet their obligations, and as long as you are a member you will have to pay annual dues? Yes____ No____

38.) Do you understand that you will be required to meet certain dress code requirements when attending Lodge? Yes ____ No ____

39.) Does your spiritual framework include the doctrine or belief in a Supreme Being or Higher Power? Yes ____ No ____

40.) Do you understand that there are no guaranteed financial or other benefits of any kind to be derived for yourself or your family from the Masonic Fraternity? Yes____ No____

41.) Do you understand that you will be required to commit certain portions of information to memory in order to advance through the degrees of Masonry? Yes____ No____

42.) Do you understand that although it is not required, you are expected to attend every regular Lodge communication so long as it does not conflict with your duty to your family, your employment, your religion, or your country, and that if unable attend, you are to notify the Lodge Secretary as to the reason? Yes_____ No_____

43.) Please list the Names, Address and Telephone numbers of three reputable persons as references. Name only people who you have known for at least three years. If you list a person you have known less than three years please explain. (*Do not include family members or persons living outside of the United States.*)

1._____
2._____
3._____

Continue to next page.

Petitioner Certification

I, _____, certify
that the entries made by me in or on this form, and on
additional sheets or pages are true, complete, and correct to
the best of my knowledge and belief, and are made in my
good faith. I also understand that a known, misleading and/or
false statement on this form can and will be just cause for the
result of my rejection as a candidate for membership in this
Lodge.

_____
Signature of the Petitioner

Date: _____

Questions for Petitioner Interview

1) Tell us about yourselves and your family.

2) Other than the information we gave you, what have you read or heard about Freemasonry?

3) There are several reasons why men join us – desire for spiritual or esoteric knowledge, interest in history, enjoyment of ritual and drama, fraternal camaraderie – what is it you hope to get out of Freemasonry?

4) What is it you think you would bring to Freemasonry?

5) What do your wife and family think about Freemasonry? Would she/they be okay with you being out once a week for lodge activities? Would they be interested in participating in Masonic family events?

6) What other clubs or organizations do you belong to? How active are you in them? If not, why not? How would Freemasonry be different?

7) What are you hobbies?

Are you willing and able to make the time, money and energy commitments we have described to you? How will you make time for it in today's busy lifestyles?

www.ingramcontent.com/pod-product-compliance
Lightning Source LLC
Chambersburg PA
CBHW071229290326
41931CB00037B/2480